D0027343

Secrets of a Special Education Advocate:

Supercharge Your Child's Special Ed IEP So Your Child Can Excel

DISCARD

Yael Cohen, M.A.

LONDON PUBLIC LIBRARY
20 EAST FIRST STREET
LONDON OH 43140   9/18

Designed, edited, and produced by Get IEP Help, Get IEP Tips, & Special Ed IEP Help. Special thanks to Ailsa Wonnacott and Bev Jones for generously sharing their knowledge bases over the years.

Limits of Liability/Disclaimer of Warranty:

As the writer and publisher, I have prepared this book to the best of my ability, however, I make no representations nor warranties as to the accuracy, applicability, or completeness of this book. I disclaim any warranty (expressed or implied), merchantability, or appropriateness for a specific purpose as I cannot account your child's situation, your school staff, how you might use the information, or even what tone of voice you may deliver it in. Neither the writer nor publisher, under any circumstances, shall be held liable for any loss or other damages of any kind. The writer and publisher is a special education advocate, and is not an attorney; the book is educational and is not intended to be legal advice. As always, the information is not intended to substitute for obtaining competent legal or other professional counsel of your own. Neither the writer nor the publisher warrant the performance, effectiveness or applicability of any sites listed in this book. All links are for informational purposes only and are not warranted for content, accuracy, or any other implied or explicit purpose. This manual contains material protected under International and Federal Copyright Laws and Treaties. Any unauthorized reprint or use of this material is prohibited. The information provided in the book or on associated websites may not reflect current legal changes.

Secrets of a Special Education Advocate

Supercharge Your Child's Special Ed IEP So Your Child Can Excel

Copyright © 2015 Yael Cohen

Contact at: 303 800-4118 or yael@getiephelp.com

All Rights Reserved. Designed, edited, and produced by Get IEP Help LLC and websites *getiephelp.com* & *www.specialediephelp.com*

To Alonit, Eliav, Jacob, & Lily,
my amazing children & their wonderful spouses, for their love and support
To Angela, the secret reader who first taught me not to believe in IQ scores
And how important advocates are
To all my colleagues & teachers, who have arrived in so many different forms
And to all those children and their parents who have trusted me to
Make a difference in their lives

About the Author

Helping parents like you find resources in and out of school, and advocate for your children's needs is exactly what Yael Cohen, MA in Special Education and BS in Speech Pathology, has for almost 30 years. In addition, Yael has spent over 35 years teaching children and youth with special challenges. She has worked both in the US and Israel. Yael has adult twin children and lives in Boulder, Colorado, where she is a member of a small working goat milking co-op. Once she started hanging out with the goats, she realized that dealing with their behaviors often has a lot of similarities to working with IEP teams and school district administrations! (Only kidding!) You can contact her by going to the website *www.specialediephelp.com or calling her at (303) 800-4118 or through her facebook page Get IEP Help.*

Contents

Introduction: Includes 1st Ten Secrets
SO DON'T SKIP THIS PART!!!

Well Hi! I'm so very glad you're here!

Looking back over the last almost 30 years of advocating for and working with kids with learning challenges, things have changed quite a bit. New laws, new rules, more complicated disabilities, segregated classes, mainstreaming, inclusion, constantly changing special education administrations, brand new teachers and some of my favorites who have retired, some terrible reading programs and some excellent ones, more onerous paperwork, and connectivity on the internet including closed groups with like-minded people to consult and collaborate with.

What hasn't changed is my biggest secret of all – shhhhh! Actually tell all parents.

Secret A:
When at all possible, it pays to resolve differences with the schools without delving into the legal system.

This is not to say that we don't need highly-qualified special education attorneys and the parents who are willing to push those insane cases where school districts just won't do the right thing, because we do need them — they have given the rest of us many invaluable resources! However, if schools and district special education administrators are willing to talk and to work with you, most of what your kids need can be attainable without the headaches, heartaches, and expense of legal action. One of the things I am most proud of as a special education advocate is that I have resolved practically all of my cases without ever mentioning a law. (I am not an attorney, so I have to be careful about practicing law without a license, but I usually find it's not necessary to even quote the law, if you can get everyone to focus on the child's needs.) More on this later . . .

I had no aspirations of becoming a Special Ed Advocate when completing my B.A. in Speech Pathology (with a focus on language development); in fact, I hardly knew this position existed, but for Angela, who was a 9 year old first grader at my internship, after an advocate intervened in her education. Angela was tested at age 4 by a psychologist because of a congenital syndrome, and with an IQ of 25 (ok, they tested her in English and she only spoke Italian), she was routed into a class for children with severe and profound needs for the next four years. The advocate had insisted she get tested again at age 8, and miraculously, she scored 40 points higher (which was also probably inaccurate, although by then she spoke English). I'm not sure whose severe and profound needs they were describing, as unbeknownst to her teachers, Angela taught herself to read — something I discovered on the day I tested her for entry into our clinic, when she picked up my tester's manual and started to read it aloud. "Ha! This child had everyone fooled!" After proving this to her new and disbelieving 1st grade teacher, Angela "learned to read overnight" and flourished!

Secret B:
Don't believe everything the testing says about your kid.

After graduating and then living and working with children with special needs (in Hebrew!) in Israel for several years, I returned to the States to continue my education with the hope of impacting the ramifications of disabilities and learning challenges early on. Luckily, what I learned in my M.A. special education program applied from early on in a child's life and well-beyond. My Masters program focused on cross-training us in a variety of professions, and put us on a school district special education track; program graduates were getting jobs either as special ed teachers, as program coordinators, or as special education administrators.

Within a year or so after finishing, and another shorter stint overseas, I accidentally discovered I could advocate for a living in the US! What fun to work for the "other side" — for the child, without the constraints of all those rules the school districts had. Sadly, things were beginning to change in the school system and the days of everyone getting around the table to legitimately problem-solve were ending along with the better funding. Many of my colleagues were becoming gatekeepers and hated it.

Fortunately for me, while advocating and getting kids' needs filled, I've also had the privilege of simultaneously working with myriads of kids with learning challenges privately, primarily teaching them to read, write, and do math. All of that has been a tremendous help every time I work with parents and schools to meet a child's individual needs. As I tell new teams I work with, my training is like their training, I can speak the jargon, I know about programs and teaching like they do, and just like them I have a teaching license. I can keep asking for translations (that the parents need). It helps most of the time.

Secret C:
Bring someone who speaks the language if you don't.

As a special education advocate, I've mostly worked in 5 or 6 different school districts near my home, but also consult with parents around the state and around the country. I can't even count the number of teams and special ed administrators I've dealt with over the years. In the district I live in, I can think back about six directors and even more assistant directors. Unfortunately, most of my own district's directors were memorable for how terrible they were, leaving us school staffs, many of whom were and are good teachers, but not terribly well-trained in really important procedures and how to partner with parents (or advocates). As a result, the kids they taught (and their parents) suffered greatly because of this.

My first big case involving my own special ed director was an ABA (Applied Behavior Analysis) case for a 3 year old medically-fragile child with autism and was notable for the director's absence. It was the very first ABA in our state, and most of the cases around the country ended up in court at that time. All the districts in the state were following it. Talk about pressure. As I had been out of the country for some time, I first had to figure out what ABA was. Whew! I discovered it was a new name for the same training I had in school in the early 70s.

Next I spent some time calling up special education directors around the country, most of whom had been forced through the courts to utilize this data-driven scientific approach, asking if this was working and how they were funding it, as the price tag was hefty! Every one of them told me that yes, it absolutely was working, and some of them explained about how the district was at least recouping some of the funding through Medicaid. I then chatted with the parents from some of the court cases, and several attorneys who were responsible for the wins, who provided us with all the other cases from around the country. I then had a long chat with one of my local and favorite special ed attorneys, who went over everything I needed to know and do for a case that was apt to end up in court. I had never worried about that before!

Secret D:
It pays to do your homework! And don't be fooled — of course it's about the money.

The meetings were the first we ever recorded, the school district sent in a cast of thousands, and we very much over-estimated the competence and preparedness of the district. We brought in two full binders of the child's data and the research, and not one person on the team bothered to even pretend to review it. Their lead "expert" — we knew he was a true expert because he literally stated that as fact 80 times in our four meetings, and I kept a tally — insisted that this child would learn by osmosis (which the parents had already tried to no avail) and would be no more than a robot if the parents continued to pursue ABA. (To foreshadow just a bit, thanks to the continuation of ABA, the child now either talks to or emails his parents, negotiating those things he hopes they will buy him.)

The doctor wrote a letter detailing the medical precautions of staff and other kids were the district to work with him in a school building and with other children. The staff pooh-poohed it, with the nurse explaining how the child was of age to grow out of the worst of it until the second meeting when only the dad came, as the child's mom was with their son in the hospital with a recurrence; the child had barely survived the night. This led to one of my best IEP meeting lines to ever deliver: "It's hard to provide FAPE (a free appropriate public education) if the child is dead. Sorry, you cannot write an IEP that will kill him."

Secret E:
Try to keep a sense of humor, as sometimes that's all you'll get.

The special education director refused to come to any of the meetings. Her absence was notable and she suddenly moved to another position in the district; her replacement refused to participate either. Every time the team made an offer of services, and we asked for their rationale, they told us it was their professional opinion. When we asked on what it was based, they simply added two hours a week until the hours were tripled over the first recommendation, but the services were still designed not to confer benefit — based on the data they were refusing to look at.

Secret F:
Ask for the staff's rationale.
You never know what you'll get.

Clearly worried about court, the district asked us to come to mediation, and not expecting a lot, I agreed if the district would order in a catered lunch, which they agreed to. Sadly, that was the only useful agreement that came out of the mediation!

Although the parents and I had conferred with their awesome special ed attorneys-to-be, and had sat for 10 hours the day before mediation as we worked to make some serious steps toward the position of the district, the district apparently had no intention of budging in our direction at all. Not an inch! We were so disillusioned and I remained wary of mediations for many years.

What happened, you may ask? The parents hired the awesome attorneys, the school district attorneys acted horribly and made the parents out to look like awful parents, and eventually, at the last moment, the district offered a sizable settlement. After agonizing at the confidentiality that curtailed their ability to make a difference for other kids too, the parents accepted the settlement, and used it to provide the ABA services needed for the next couple of years, to get their child the needed foundation to make the progress he has. While I was not privy to the numbers because of the confidentiality close, I was able to use an open records request and discover that the district had spent an obscene amount of money, approximately triple the parents' investment, to fight a 3 year old. And I objected loudly in places that mattered! (And, what I discovered is that so much for confidentiality — all the school districts knew the outcome and that helped other kids.)

Secret G:
You'd be surprised what you might be able to find out
using an open records request.

Secret H:
The school districts and their attorneys all talk
to each other - there are no secrets.

For many years, I tried to avoid the terrible special ed directors in my own district, while at the same time I had some wonderful relationships with those in other districts, depending on the director. (Fortunately, some of my own district's assistant special ed directors, at times, were pretty good.)

But hanging in there was worth it, as finally, after 25 years of waiting, finally some good and qualified people were hired to run the special ed department in my district, and they early on demonstrated their willingness to work hard to make positive changes. In their first few months, they resolved a large number of terrible ongoing situations, apologized to at least one set of parents (and what a difference that made for the parents), and jumped into training individual staffs (after watching or being alerted to errors).

What kind of errors were they seeing (and repairing) the first year in the district? Pretty much the same kinds of errors that many parents and advocates see routinely all over the country

- not individualizing plans for individual children (one size fits all)

- not understanding and applying test results and other evidence — One of my favorites was a psychologist who explained that it was acceptable that a child's scores dropped after a year of intensive teaching, explaining that we should expect a "learning curve."

- the staffs unprepared to answer the question as to if there was an impact of the disability on the child's education — and what the impact was

- no meeting agenda

- not involving the specialists working with the child

- not giving parents access to evaluation reports and draft IEPs ahead of the meeting — in fact, our new director told all schools they were to send these out a week in advance, which allows parents to participate more fully in special education meeting — and then he told parents to expect them.

- school staff not appreciating that parents are an important component of every child's special ed team and using their historical knowledge of the child.

And, the new director and assistant directors helped facilitate communication between parents and schools & between advocates and schools — which was just as important as what they did behind the scenes.

Does everyone like appreciate this set of directors as much as I do? Not everyone does. Are they perfect? No, none of us are. Does this mean we always agree? Heck no! But we can communicate and the trust that we've developed carries us through some of the hardest of situations. As I said, I've waited a long time for quality.

What does this mean for parents?

Secret I:
It means that when you can't get things resolved at the school level, that it often pays to go to the next level for help. It's often worth it to go to your special ed administrators, and sometimes even past them into district administration.

If you can do this with openness and respect, bypassing the anger that you may so rightfully experience, you can often get what your child needs without a war. Some of your administrators will be incredibly useful — partner with them. Sadly, not all of them will be so useful and some will be harmful. Try to figure it out quickly which kind they are, and make adjustments as needed.

Secret J:
Forging good relationships with your child's special education staff and when you need to, with the district administrators, is crucial for your child, and for parents and for advocates alike.

Sure, you have to stick to the child's needs (and not just once, I've been accused of being like a dog with a bone, refusing to give it up), but having a positive and trusting relationship goes a long way when things are on the verge of falling apart. Most parents & advocates are not out to "catch" the schools or district doing what's wrong, but to help them better meet the needs of students. Just like in every field, some administrators are great and others are not (and grudgingly I'll admit that not every advocate is great either, and sometimes parents get really angry and terribly offend the school staff). I shy away from those administrators who are terrible, but partner with ones who are good. As a parent, you can do this too. If you try, you may hopefully be able to find someone useful who is willing to help. It often helps to go through the channels – unless your school is terrible (in which case you should transfer), give them a heads up before you go over their heads.

This book is not all-encompassing as much of the how-to is covered in a variety of other sources, including the free videos and other gifts I'll be sending you. Instead this book focuses on some of the crucial questions that parents have asked me over and over during the years I have advocated, those painful topics that impact parents (and their children) the most. Other questions were generated from an online parent survey — be watching for some more of the surveys as they help me tailor material that you want and need the most; you'll find some of them on my facebook page: "Get IEP Help." Finally, this book also contains a lot of the secrets I have learned that can help you get what you need from school for your child with special needs.

Important Note

You will see the term "IEP" (Individual Education Plan) many times in this book. It is an abbreviation that has numerous meanings. It can refer to a document or a plan (the IEP), a team composed of you and the school professionals (the IEP team), or a meeting (the IEP meeting). No matter how it is used, it refers to the special education services and instruction to be delivered to a particular student.

SIGN UP HERE FOR YOUR FREE GIFT

Be sure to sign up right now for the free video series by going to *www.getieptips.com*. The tips address the answers to the most common how-to questions about the results you are seeking when it comes to your child learning. There are twenty-one 2 – 3 minute videos included.

Obviously, I promise not to spam you, or ever give anyone your information, and you can stop this any time you want. After you complete the daily video series, I will continue to send you additional useful info from time to time that you can put into place to help your child succeed!

Ever Felt This Way in a School Meeting About Your Child?

"I sat in that first meeting with my heart throbbing. There were at least a dozen people, most of whom I had never met, sitting on the other side of the table, telling me about my child's numbers. They kept smiling at me while they spoke—mostly in what sounded like Greek. They gave me lots of papers and told me I should sign. Although they said I'm their partner, I seemed to be the only one who didn't speak Greek or understand what the numbers meant. I was still trying to grasp what they said about something being wrong with my child. They asked me questions, but didn't ask more about my suggestions or write down what I said. I thought I knew my child, but suddenly, at that meeting, I felt stupid and left out."

or

"I've been to many special education meetings about my child, but I can't figure out why we are meeting again. It has been three years and my child still can't read, even though they keep telling me that this is the program he needs. They are saying something about my son not being entitled to a Cadillac, only to a Chevy. Don't they know all cars need gas to run?"

or

"My son has been suspended 5 times this year already and he's only seven. The school seems to think it is his fault, or my fault. I'm not sure if I should be angry or wonder if I'm missing something. What should I do?"

A Parent's Perspective

"The difference between our son's first and second initial special education eligibility meetings was like night and day. At the first meeting, it was as if we walked into a time warp and had no idea what was going to happen. My gut feeling was that what they were saying about our child didn't totally make sense. We had no idea what the testing meant or what had to be done to help him. They kept telling us what we should do and insisting that we sign, even though we had no idea what we were signing, and we didn't understand about his ability and his disability. I did some research on the internet, but I just couldn't learn it fast enough. It was a whole new field of study!

Yael, the advocate we found between the meetings, explained everything to us in language we could understand, analyzed the actual testing and the IEP (Individual Education Plan) document, asked questions, and offered solutions. We knew nothing about reading programs, but Yael convinced the school (we're still not sure quite how she did this) to use one of the major research-based reading programs to teach him. She gave us a plan to follow, got us accountability from the school, and got our son the instruction he needed. She also found us several specialists to help him outside of school. Because of her teaching background in special education, she is a walking encyclopedia and has given us so many resources!

We still bring Yael with us to meetings although we now feel like valued members of our son's team; she can talk that same language the school folks do and gets things we, and often the staff, hadn't even thought of into place. She helps to make sure everyone

– teachers, tutors, therapists – and everything is coordinated. If snags occur, she knows who to call to get a plan into action. Had we not found Yael, no doubt our son would still not be able to read or do math. She is truly a godsend."

Susan Williams, Boulder, CO

Chapter One: Requests and Denials

The Ultimate Get Help Guide

 **Hi Yael, I went to parent conferences last night and the teacher said my child is already behind. He's only in 1st grade and cries through homework every night. She said we should probably keep an eye on him. Is that enough? Or should I be pursuing something else? Please give me a call back. Thanks.**

1. How, or who, do I ask for services when my child is struggling in school?

The first thing to do is to meet with your child's regular education teacher and discuss your concerns. Take samples of your child's work to show where you see the struggles. Ask the teacher if she has noticed any learning struggles or behavioral problems in the classroom and ask what she might suggest to help your child. Ask about the services that the school might be able to provide to increase your child's success.

Sometimes a teacher may suggest that your child needs just a bit more time or another classroom approach. It is often fine to give this a chance as long as there is a date (a month to six weeks) to take another look at progress. In many school districts, this is now called RTI or Response to Intervention, and usually consists of extra help (that may even be given by the Special Ed teacher). Note that all school districts received a clarification notice from the US Department of Education reminding them that they may not use RTI to delay a special education evaluation, so it's really up to you if you want to see how it will work. RTI and a special education evaluation can run simultaneously and information from RTI can be used as part of the evaluation. However, if you and/or the teacher feel either now, or at the next meeting, that there may be a deeper learning issue, you should request a special education evaluation—in writing! Once you make the request, dated and in writing, the clock starts running and the school/district must meet certain deadlines to test your child and meet with you (at an IEP/Special Education meeting) to discuss those results. Be sure to keep a copy of your dated request.

Secret K:
It's usually better to start the conversation with your child's teacher – that's probably the person who knows him the best of all at school.

---

2. If everyone thinks that my son needs help, what is the process?

It's a great start that everyone agrees that your son needs help. Your next move is to arrange a meeting with the special education teacher at the school to discuss evaluating your child. The teacher will ask you to sign a form giving them permission to evaluate. The form will list the kinds of evaluations in areas of suspected disability the school plans to do. You will want to understand as much as possible about these evaluations before you sign the permission, so ask questions or check with an out-of-school professional. Give the teacher copies of any documentation you have from medical professionals and care providers, along with any input from friends or family about your child's strengths and difficulties. It is important to be open, but you are not required to share details that make you uncomfortable, or to disclose anything you would not want to see in your child's school file. (There's nothing so embarrassing to a teenager sitting in his high school IEP meeting than to read about his history of wetting his pants.) And, although doctors often write on their notes to contact them if there is a need for more information, the school needs your written permission for that. Generally I tell parents to have the school put questions they may have in writing, and the parents can ask the doctor to write a response – less confusion that way.

The evaluation will be done at school by a team of specialists which could include a special education teacher, a school psychologist, an occupational therapist (OT), and a speech and language therapist (SPL/SLP/ST). You will be notified in writing of an Individualized Education Plan (IEP or

Eligibility) meeting, at which all the information collected will be discussed to determine if your son is eligible for special education services. If he is found eligible, the information will be used to determine what needs to happen in school to help him and what the goals are for the coming year. It will then be used to decide what services, accommodations, and modifications he will need. If the child is not found eligible for special education, he or she may still be eligible for some extra help. (See Evaluation Chapter (10) first on what to do if your child is not found eligible for Special Education.)

Many school districts provide a separate Evaluation Report. Whether they do or don't, all the evaluation information will go into an IEP (Individual Education Plan). An IEP is like a contract stating what the school district agrees to do for your child in the coming year. The evaluations can be long and complicated, so when signing permission for the school to evaluate, ask to receive copies of everything, including reports and a draft IEP (if prepared) a week before the meeting so you can read and digest everything. Write a list of your thoughts and questions about the evaluations so that you are prepared to ask them at the meeting. Make sure you really understand the information, or find someone independent who can help you with it, because is the only way that you can truly involved in creating a good plan for your child.

Secret L:
It is important to be open, but you are not required to share details that make you uncomfortable, or to disclose anything you would not want to see in your child's school file.

---

3. The school disagreed with the doctor, the day care, and us about the need to test our daughter. What should we do?

It must be very confusing to hear different recommendations for your daughter. It is important to make your request for an evaluation in writing as then the school is forced to evaluate or to take you to a hearing. (Special education directors have told me it's a lot cheaper to just do the evaluation.) Give this request to the school principal and your daughter's classroom teacher. Include detailed descriptions from doctors, day care personnel, and yourself explaining exactly what you are observing, so that the school understands your concerns and the reason for your request. Ask the school to share any observations they have about your daughter in school, so that you understand what they are seeing and why they may be saying no to evaluations. This might be easier to do in a meeting, but you always want to document, even if it's after-the-fact.

If they refuse to consider testing your child, they must provide you with a written notice of their refusal and their reasoning within a realistic timeline (often considered as soon as possible or within 15 days). This may be included in "Prior Written Notice (PWN)." They will also have to give you a document informing you of your due process rights; it is crucial that you read it carefully. (This does not mean you have to file for due process – there's a lot to do before that.)

Secret M:
If you really want to ensure that your child receives an evaluation, you must put your request in writing so that it's really clear, and the clock starts ticking.

---

4. If the IEP is in place for my child and I feel as if there has been no improvement, how can I get another meeting without waiting for the annual IEP date?

It sounds like you want some clarification and reassurance about how your child is doing at school. Make a list of all your observations and concerns about your child's progress. Then list any questions you have and any requests you want to make. Don't forget to list and acknowledge anything you feel is working at school; this is equally as important as what is not working. Then, request an IEP review meeting (in writing). You are allowed to do this at any time; in fact, anyone on the team can do that.

At the meeting, first share everything you are pleased with, and then your concerns, questions, and requests. State any ideas that you have, and then ask the school for their observations and ideas. Your goal is to get agreement on the action the school will take to either try new things, or measure progress in a way that is more useful to you. It is often helpful to speak to parents of other kids with learning challenges or an advocate, to figure out how to best work with the school team to make changes, monitor progress, and ensure your child's success.

5. My child was denied special education services in one school district but was approved in another less than a year later. Is there anything that can be done against the first school district?

I can understand your confusion and anger about the decision of the first school district. Some school districts seem to have arbitrary rules. Others use outdated methods and may believe that your child must be two years behind grade level before they will take action. Using this method, they could take a few years until the gap between your child and other children becomes big enough for the school district to consider him eligible for special education services. (This was the whole purpose of RTI services.)

And, yes, you are right in thinking that it is silly to wait another six months or a year to get help. (If you were still in the first school district, we would suggest that you follow the recommendations outlined in this book to get your child special education services.) Other schools/districts may be more lenient about making a "clinical decision" in which the numbers may not exactly work out, but the team decides to grant services anyway. Unfortunately, it would probably be a very difficult, lengthy, and costly battle to prove that your child's disability did not increase in the period of a year or that the first team was wrong. Your efforts might be better spent in making sure that your child is receiving the appropriate services in the current school, and continues to thrive and improve.

Sign Up Here For Your Free Gift
Be sure to sign up right now for the free video series by going to www.getieptips.com . The tips address the answers to the most common how-to questions about the results you are seeking when it comes to your child learning. There are twenty-one 2 - 3 minute videos included.

Chapter Two: Simplifying the IEP

Working Too Hard? Simplifying the Process

Hello, Yael? My daughter is in 4th grade, has been on an IEP since 1st grade, and has made absolutely no progress since that time. She can't read, write, or do math, and comes home and melts down every single evening. I have to force her to get on the bus. The team gives me the impression that it's all her fault. Nothing I say seems to matter, even though I used to be a teacher myself. How do I get her the help she needs? Please call me at your earliest convenience.

6. Every year, I go to my child's IEP meeting and it seems to be a waste of time. The meeting is disorganized and we never seem to accomplish any thing. What can I do?

This kind of disorganization is quite common, unfortunately, and it does not help you feel like you are really involved and able to advocate for your child. Sometimes the problem is that no one is effectively facilitating the meeting because the school staff is not necessarily skilled at this. If that is the case, you can help out. The IEP meeting is a process with fairly clear steps. It will help if you know what these steps are, so you can use your expertise as a parent to make good educational decisions for your child. Ask the special education teacher to send you an agenda a week before the meeting.

For an "annual review" meeting, the agenda should include such things as introductions, current levels of performance (how your child is doing in school), progress on old goals, development of new goals, decisions about how much and what services, and decisions about what accommodations he should have. For a "Triennial IEP" or an "Eligibility IEP" meeting (held every three years), the meeting should also include reviewing evaluations, deciding if he is still eligible for special education services -- and which services -- and deciding what assistance he needs.

When you get the agenda, spend some time writing out everything that you want to say about each item. Let the special education teacher know other topics you would like to include. If the teacher does not send home an agenda, prepare your own and take it with you. Ask if the teacher will make copies of the agenda for everyone who might be attending the meeting; if that's a problem, you can always offer to do that. Take someone with you to the meeting who can take notes and help get the group back on track if they start to wander. If the time runs out and you have not covered all the agenda items, ask for a second meeting to finish the process. If you are as organized as possible and pleasant with your intentions, you have a better chance of having a successful meeting.

Although many parents are somewhat intimidated by going up the ladder, when you have a team which is not functioning well, or if you feel cannot provide the direction for your child, unless the special education administration has a terrible reputation, I often will request that a district special ed coordinator, or assistant director (even the director sometimes) attend the meeting. Sometimes I do this through the special education teacher, and sometimes I approach the district administration directly and invite them to attend. I have found that very often, administrators help resolve situations in which staff is not prepared, or may not know what to do – and I love it that I get the first shot of filling them in on the situation.

Secret N:
Someone has to be organized in chaotic meetings;
if no one else is going to step up, go ahead!

---

7. Who is supposed to write the IEP for children with special needs?

It's a team effort. The team is made up of YOU (the parent, and mentioned first by Congress), at least one of your child's regular education teachers, the specialists who provide testing and services, (if possible) the paraeducators who work directly with the child, school administrators, and sometimes a district administrator. Your input and suggestions are vital when making decisions about goals for your child, what services will be provided, how they will be provided, and what is needed for your child. An advocate, friend, or family member who attends the meeting with you is also part of the IEP Team and can help decide what goes into the IEP.

There may also be medical information that is critical and provided by the child's physician; while the doctor may not need to be at the meeting, he/she is also part of the child's team. Usually, the school specialists write up their own portions of the IEP, and the special education teacher is responsible for writing up and finalizing the document. A lot of schools are willing to project the IEP document on the wall and make changes in real time, so you can see them go in, or be removed. (You'll still want them to print you out a copy before you leave the meeting.)

Secret O:
You are an integral part of the team; don't let yourself get sidelined. You may not have a degree in special education, but don't fool yourself – you have information about your child that no one else does.

---

8. The IEP team couldn't agree – especially me. The district would like to bring in a mediator. Should I agree and what qualifications should the mediator have?

You sound worried about how much power you will have in this kind of situation. We imagine you're also thinking that something could be forced upon you and your child. Mediation is voluntary, and you do not have to agree to mediate. You don't have to remain at the mediation if it is going poorly. Agreements reached and signed at mediation are generally binding, so ask ahead of time. Mediation does not cost you anything and could result in a compromise agreement you can live with.

Generally, the state contracts with and pays for the mediator. States are required to have a list of people who are qualified mediators and knowledgeable about special education laws and regulations. In some states, administrative law judges are used as mediators; on the other hand, you might discover it's the special education director from the neighboring district (possibly not so unbiased). Mediators must not have a personal or professional interest that conflicts with their ability to be unbiased, which hopefully gives parents some reassurance. (Do realize that often district special education administration and the mediators do get to see each other, even often, and you may observe some friendly interactions between them.)

There are no national qualifications for mediators, but most have had some form of specific mediation training in addition to at least some knowledge about special education. Mediators usually will give you a copy of their qualifications; if not, ask for it. We suggest that you speak to an advocate before deciding about mediation. An advocate may be able to help you negotiate with the school without the need for a mediator by getting the right people in the room, or may be able to attend mediation with you.

You still have a right to use legal remedies if mediation fails, however, most likely you will be asked to sign a form stating that no settlement offer or discussions held in mediation can be used in legal proceedings (unless you can discover it another way). You should clarify with the mediator what confidentiality means prior to it starting, especially what you can and can't say to family and/or friends who know you have been disagreeing with the school. It is very important to be extremely well organized before you go into mediation. You want to be clear, and list, exactly what the problems are and potential solutions to resolving them. For example, if the teacher refuses to communicate with you, then a different solution might be that an alternate staff person will communicate with you. A mediator will generally meet with you prior to the mediation to gather information; this is your chance to state what it is you are hoping to achieve in mediation. You will also have the opportunity during mediation to have private conversations with the mediator. We have generally felt it has been useful to be open and clear with the mediator.

Sometimes, we've been very creative in mediations. I always have the parents bring a nice-sized photo of the child and we leave that on the table. It needs to be clear whose life we are discussing. One time, a parent culled through the audios of the meetings on her child (and yes, the school was well aware we were taping), and we got to play clips of almost all the participants agreeing that they had not been able to meet the child's needs. That definitely helped. (The parent framed it as "We're already mostly in agreement.")

I have been to mediations that have been wonderful and others that have been worthless. It all depends who is attending and how willing they are to compromise. Last year I had a director join the team at an IEP meeting and we got everything fixed up prior to the mediation. (That makes it easy!) I've also been in mediations without a mediator – it worked just to have the right people in the room. In general, it helps if you can figure out ahead of time what you can live with; on the other hand, there are sometimes things you might not be able to budge on. Give it some thought. And hope the school district does that too!

Secret P:
When everyone is open to compromise,
mediation can be a much more viable process
than ending up in the legal system,
and really – you have nothing much to lose!

---

9. Can we get rid of our daughter's IEP?

It used to be the case that once you signed the original consent for special education services that all decision-making deferred to the team (including you, but no more so than anyone else). So if you wanted to then reject your child being in special education, you had to convince the team as a whole. I remember hearing at conferences that some school districts were even taking parents to due process hearings over this when the district did not agree with the parent removing their child from services and that the law didn't say much about this. (Usually it's parents who take school districts to due process over not giving services so this was surprising.)

In 2008, the US Department of Education changed the rules to say that a parent could remove a child from special education. However, if you then want your child to again receive services, you have to start at the beginning with a new evaluation. In addition, there is no guarantee that he or she will get services or accommodations under a 504 plan if you have revoked special education services.

So, if you want to remove your child from special education, consider the ramifications – both good and bad – and if so, put it in writing.

10. Should my son attend an IEP meeting? If so, at what age do you suggest he start coming?

I know quite a few students, including some with significant disabilities, who have been very effective at explaining their needs at their IEP meetings.

If your child is capable of understanding his needs and is able to communicate those needs to others, then he should have a voice in the meeting. It can be very powerful when a student with a good understanding of his own abilities and disabilities can convey what he needs to team members. Middle school, or certainly high school age, is an appropriate time to start participating, but this depends on your child. If your child would like to attend, it would be a good idea to discuss the appropriateness of his participation, and any supports that he will need, from you or from the special education staff. Some students appreciate coming for just a piece of the meeting – to say hi and make a comment about how things are going. Some parents gather information from their child before the meeting and act as ambassador at the meeting if the child really wants to be heard, but finds meetings with a bunch of adults intimidating. Personally, I do not recommend a student's presence if we suspect there will be conflict at the meeting. In that case, they should be left out of the meeting.

Secret Q:
Do NOT let your child become a pawn
in a disagreement you have with the school staff.
Your child has to go back to class with them later!

---

11. I have a middle school daughter on an IEP and would like to know how to get all her teachers at the IEP meeting. One teacher refuses to go along with any accommodations.

It is often difficult to get all the teachers at one time and the school is not required to make them all attend the IEP meeting. This is especially true at the secondary school level. If you are having problems with one teacher, specifically ask for that teacher to attend the meeting as the regular education representative. Send your request in writing to both the principal and the special education teacher.

We have also found it useful for parents to send a personal invitation to the teacher (actually to all the student's teachers) and have your daughter deliver it if she feels comfortable doing so. Make this request well in advance of the IEP meeting, so that the school can arrange coverage for all the teachers who will be at the meeting. Mention that you are providing a snack – and do that. No, it's not your job to feed them, but we have found that this kindness can go a long way.

In addition, at the start of every school year, touch base with each of her teachers through a short conference, or sending an email or a personal note (in a nice card) with a photo of your child, along with a list of the accommodations. Make it brief and be clear that you will be available to collaborate with each of them during the year. Use your parent-teacher conferences to your advantage by discussing any successes or difficulties that have arisen. Write up some questions for each teacher before the meeting and ask them about how specific classroom accommodations are working out. It's a nice way of alerting them, in case they haven't gotten the message, that your child does have accommodations.

While proofreading this final copy, I was alerted to a situation in which the accommodation of being provided with a study guide, or road map, at the beginning of every unit was finally written into one of my student's IEP. All teachers but one were complying. (I know one teachers who was re-quired to start doing this for one child; he found all his kids did better with this assistance, and now he provides it to them all.) As for the one teacher who refused the accommodation, the mother was tired of complaining and wondering what to do next. We talked about working her way up the ladder and inviting key school and district special ed staff to the IEP meet-ing about this – whether the teacher came or not. Eventually, the teacher agreed. A future step would have been a state complaint, so I'd be sure to record the meeting as you probably will need proof.

Sign Up Here For Your Free Gift
Be sure to sign up right now for the free video series by going to www.getieptips.com . The tips address the answers to the most common how-to questions about the results you are seeking when it comes to your child learning. There are twenty-one 2 - 3 minute videos included.

Chapter Three: Meeting Technicalities

Should They Or Shouldn't They?

Hi Yael, I discovered at the meeting that the school had already changed my child's service hours several weeks before the meeting, and hadn't even told me. Now they are insisting on a day and time that I simply cannot meet with them. What should I do? Call me back please!

12. Can the school hold meetings about my child without my being there?

Often school personnel will gather to discuss testing and results among the team members, but they should not have an official meeting to determine your child's placement or the manner that the services will be provided without the parent, parents' designated representative, or a "surrogate" parent in attendance. Does that ever happen? Yes, it does, and when you suspect it has happened, you should insist, verbally and in writing, that a full discussion of the issues and decisions related to your child also occur in your presence.

Politely notify the team in writing that you are calling for an IEP meeting and that any changes that were made without you are void. Schools are supposed to make all reasonable efforts to hold IEP meetings when it is convenient for a parent to attend. Sometimes everyone will be willing to come early in the morning, or stay late in the afternoon, to hold a meeting. Most staff are not willing to hold meetings at 2am, so try to be flexible.

Although it is not really my first choice because of the technological difficulties still, many of us are able to attend IEP meetings via video through an app like Skype or Facetime, or just a conference call. If you do use technology to attend, be sure to monitor volume with those present as it can be difficult to hear, or you may be perceived as shouting when you aren't. In addition, make sure to have a copy of the draft of the IEP ahead of time so you can truly participate in the meeting. Ask everyone to speak up!

13. If the annual IEP meeting is delayed because we can't come to an agreement on a date, do my son's services keep going until we meet?

It is not uncommon for an IEP meeting to be delayed beyond the annual date on which it should be held. In these situations, the IEP, which is already in place, and any services it includes, continues to be implemented until the IEP team can meet and develop a new IEP. This means that there will be no interruption in the services and supports your son receives in school despite the ending dates quoted in the current IEP.

If a delay is needed, you may be asked to sign a delay notice by the school. This notice will serve as a record that the IEP team agreed to delay the meeting, so that the school district does not appear, on record, to be failing to hold the IEP within the required timeline. You are also able to write across the IEP (or on a separate piece of paper if the IEP is on a computer) that although the IEP is not finished, you agree to allow the school to implement certain new services (and name them), but that you do not agree with the IEP as written. Add that another meeting is to be scheduled to finish the IEP. This does not work if you have not signed the original IEP and consent for services.

Secret R:
If the school/district has acted in poor faith (like a recent case I have where the district special ed coordinator waltzed in and informed the mom that they would do this with or without her), don't sign. Truly, the most that will happen is that they'll get their hand slapped, but you'll feel better!

---

14. Are participants in an annual IEP meeting required to sign in? Does this mean we are agreeing to the IEP?

All participants who attend the IEP meeting should sign the document that verifies that they were at the meeting. No, you are not agreeing to anything that is in the IEP just because you signed that you were at the meeting. (Just check what you are signing.) Some states are now requiring an extra signature on the determination of disability form of everyone who is in the meeting. Although technically a parent only has to sign once for consent for one's child to receive special education services, some states have more stringent rules about signatures. Check your state rules.

Secret S:
Except for the participation form, you do not have to sign anything you are not comfortable with in a special education meeting. You can always tell them that you are going to read it over at home and will get back with them – and then do please – within a day or so, or reject it, and call for another meeting. In fact, if you don't take an advocate who can carefully monitor what goes in, definitely don't sign until you have time to digest it. Oh, and the school can always open up a new meeting form, even if they "finalize" the document.

---

15. Should I sign the finished IEP?

First, parents generally only sign special education consent forms for permission for the school to evaluate (or reevaluate), and to give consent for their child to receive special education services when the first IEP is written. Sometimes schools ask you to sign subsequent IEPs. If they insist on your signing, you can ask them to point out where in the federal (or state) law it says you must sign. (Some states do require that parents sign all IEPs.) We suggest you do not sign if you don't agree with the document or if it is not finished, but if your state insists, you can sign with a statement above your signature which states any disagreements you have with the document. (This is now more difficult as almost all IEPs are on computers, so you may have to follow up with an email – chances are you can do that right on your smart phone before you leave the room.) You will, however, want to be certain that every IEP is actually complete and accurate: the goals, objectives, and the services/time allotted make sense, your concerns are noted, and proper accommodations and modifications are included to meet your child's educational needs.

We suggest that you take a copy of all documentation and paperwork from the meeting home with you, and then get back to the IEP team with your written input. Include what you agree with and what you don't agree with. If you are feeling apprehensive, I suggest you retain the services of an advocate to look over the IEP and make sure that it appears in order before you consent.

No matter what you are told otherwise, you do NOT have to sign even the initial IEP at the meeting; you can take the document home to read, or get a consultation on it. Your child cannot receive special education services until you do sign the first IEP consent form, but this does not mean the school cannot do anything else in the interim – it just will not be special education. When there is a disagreement about a portion of the services to be provided, I encourage parents to write a note right on the IEP if possible, or to put in writing, a statement saying you agree only to a specified portion of the services to take place. (Of course, this will not work if this is an initial IEP.) Add to your statement that another meeting will be held to finish the IEP. (Be sure to get a copy of all paperwork before leaving.)

Secret T:
Don't allow yourself to be intimidated. This is about your kid. When I first started out in the field, someone told me about research that said that parents at an IEP meeting really only hear the first 5 or so minutes, and if they say something bad about your kid? You don't even absorb that much. Take the documents home, read them and come back with any questions you have.

---

16. I went to my 6th grade son's IEP meeting and noted that none of the regular educators were present. When I asked, I was told that the special education teacher had talked to them all and could share the information, as they were all busy. I thought a regular education teacher had to be at the meeting. Am I right?

You are right. If your son is in regular education classes, then one of his regular education teachers needs to be at the IEP meeting. This is crucial, as the general education teacher will often have insights that the special education providers do not. The school is not required to have all of your child's regular education teachers present and may have the absent teachers provide input in writing. If a regular education teacher is not present when the meeting begins, remind the special education teacher or administrator that you want a representative from regular education to attend. (You might even be asked to sign an excusal form and probably shouldn't.) You can ask that one of the teachers be arranged immediately. If you are told that this is not possible, tell the school participants that you wish to reschedule the meeting for a time when a regular educator can be present. This will often lead to the school quickly figuring out how to cover the class so the regular educator may attend the meeting.

Even though we were told it is impossible, we've had some pretty good luck attracting secondary school teachers to attend by scheduling the IEP meeting right after school (or during the team planning period), and sending a written invitation to all the student's regular teachers two weeks prior to the meeting. Be sure to mention how important you feel each teacher's input is. For those who are unable to attend, you can request that they send you their observations and ideas before the meeting. If you have specific questions for the teachers, you can include these in your invitation. Most teachers care a lot and some have thanked us for including them.

It is also important for you to attend any parent-teacher conferences that are offered. Prepare some questions to ask, because this is your opportunity to talk to all your child's regular teachers for at least a few minutes. Ask how your child is doing in class, which accommodations in your child's IEP have been most helpful, and what recommendations they have for supports for your child which are not currently in the IEP. This is always a good way to find out if teachers know what accommodations are in the IEP, and, second, if they notice your child in class to the extent that they have some ideas about how they could be even more successful in teaching him.

17. What happens if the school forges an IEP?

Oh yes, this can happen! (I've had it happen a few times.) If you suspect that the school has forged any information on the IEP, or signatures of persons that were, or were not, in attendance, you should contact your special education director and/or your state Department of Education and ask to speak to an advisor to resolve this matter. I've most often seen this when kids are suddenly staffed out of special education services. If you are in possession of any documentation that shows a discrepancy in the paperwork for the IEP, you should have copies of it available when you contact your state Department of Education. Or, please feel free to contact me, and I will be happy to consider options.

18. Should the special education teacher be the sole decision maker in placing a child in special education and should it be based only on the test scores?

It is the IEP team as a whole that should be making decisions about your child's eligibility for special education. The team includes: you, the parent; anyone else with knowledge about your child who you wish to invite to the meeting; a special education teacher; a regular education teacher; and the school personnel who did the evaluations with your child (so that you can get answers to your questions). It is not appropriate for any one person to make this decision. The team should use the information gathered by the evaluations along with information from you and your child's teachers about classroom performance to decide whether your child meets the criteria for special education eligibility. The most critical piece is if there is an impact on the disability on the child's education – if there is not, and there is not a need for specialized instruction, then a child will not be found eligible for special education. Again, the parent must sign consent for initial placement in special education, and the team cannot force a parent to do so.

Secret U:
It doesn't matter how friendly you and your child's team are; if it's not in writing, it didn't happen!

Sign Up Here For Your Free Gift
Be sure to sign up right now for the free video series by going to www.getieptips.com . The tips address the answers to the most common how-to questions about the results you are seeking when it comes to your child learning. There are twenty-one 2 - 3 minute videos included.

Chapter Four: Implementation

Isn't Anyone Going to Do Anything?

 Hi Yael, my child's teacher just informed me that she really doesn't really know what my child can do and that she doesn't have much time for my kid. It's a couple of months into the school year. She also told me that she has no help from the special education team. Now what?

19. What can we do when the school is not teaching our child and not implementing the IEP? In particular, getting the assistive technology in place for our child is taking forever. What is a reasonable timeline to get everything in place?

Once the IEP team has met and created an IEP for your child, there should be little delay in getting all requirements of the IEP in place. Many items, such as special education teacher services and most accommodations, can be put in place the next day. Of course, there may be delays in getting more complicated services in place. Unfortunately, I have found assistive technology to be one of the services that often takes longer. This seems to be because of the complex nature of some of the technology needed, thoughtful decision-making and possible unavoidable delays in receiving it.

If you can work with the school to get everything in place as soon as possible, this is the best strategy. If there is an unreasonable delay, you might consider calling a meeting to create an action plan, which will outline everything that needs to happen, who is responsible for getting it done, and a reasonable time line by which it will be completed. Alternatively, you could ask the school team to create the action plan and send it to you for review.

In the meantime, it is essential that you make a record of any proof you have that your child is not being taught, or that the IEP is not being implemented. You may not need this information, but if the delays continue, you may want to consider using it to request services to compensate for those lost due to this delay. If you do ultimately take this action, you will need to request these compensatory services in writing.

20. Who is responsible for implementing the IEP?

Technically, the school district is responsible for making sure the IEP is implemented. The day-to-day support is the responsibility of all the adults who work with your child in the school, but their roles will differ depending on their area of expertise. If your child receives time from the special education teacher, this teacher is usually responsible for drafting the IEP (based upon the IEP team's direction), modifying the curriculum, providing direct or in-class teaching, supervising any paraeducators who work with your child, and consulting with other school staff. The "related service" providers, such as occupational and speech/language therapists, are responsible for delivering their specialized services and consulting with other school staff. All adults in the school, including regular educators, are responsible for providing your child with all the accommodations that are in the IEP. It's a bit like an orchestra with the special education teacher as the conductor.

The more organized and focused everyone is in the IEP meeting, the better, because then you can help keep things on track in the meeting and throughout the year. When you go to IEP meetings, ask to review the written wording of agreements reached before you leave the room, so you are clear who is going to do what. If you do not get this (usually because the time runs out), follow up with a letter clearly stating the agreements. That will help you keep track of whether things have happened, and you will know who to go to if you think there is a problem. And, if you have an issue, go first to that person and you can then follow up with the principal. Try hard not to jump over people without at least talking with them.

21. When are long-term goals and short-term objectives both needed in an IEP?

Previously, schools had to write a year's worth of both goals and short-term objectives (some of the steps to be accomplished on the way to achieving the goal). Currently, only long-term goals are necessary in an IEP, except when a child has a significant disability and is assessed using alternative tests as opposed to those given annually to all kids in the state.

Objectives make sense for kids who need to learn skills in a structured way, with small steps built in (scaffolding), because the short-term objectives break the larger goals down into smaller pieces which are both easier to measure and to use to show progress. For this reason, some schools still write both goals and objectives. In either case, they must be measurable.

Most parents and advocates like having short-term objectives because it lets everyone know that the child is truly making progress that is observable, which is much better than an end-of-the-year surprise of not meeting the goal.

Secret V:
Make sure the goal doesn't happen only once.
Have the goals end with wording such as
"3x a day, for a period of 3 consecutive school weeks."

Sign Up Here For Your Free Gift
Be sure to sign up right now for the free video
series by going to www.getieptips.com . The tips
address the answers to the most common how-to
questions about the results you are seeking when
it comes to your child learning. There are
twenty-one 2 - 3 minute videos included.

Chapter Five: Behavior

I'm Trying Hard Not To Take This Personally, But You're Talking About My Child

Hi Yael, My son is about to get suspended again, and maybe placed into a separate school for kids who are behavior problems. That would be really bad since this is the only school that has ever taught him how to read. Apparently he freaked out when they gave him some command and ran outside the school. Oh, and did I tell you that the doctor has been changing his medications for the last two months? Please call me back.

22. The school has suspended my son twice for hurting other kids. He has sensory integration disorder and he often hurts people accidentally. The school does not seem to acknowledge this, nor do they have any idea how to help him. At every meeting, the principal spends most of the time reading me a list of all my son's negative behaviors. This leaves no time to share any ideas about how to help him. What can I do?

There is plenty you can do. The first thing is to request, in writing, that the school perform a functional behavior assessment (usually called an FBA); they may need to bring in a specialist from the district or the state to help them do this. The first step of this process is to figure out what your child is trying to achieve by his behaviors, or as it is often stated, the function of the behaviors. To do this, the team (including you) will need to determine on which of your son's behaviors to take data. The description of those behaviors should be very clear about exactly what those behaviors look like. (See Question 25 for more detailed information on this topic.) An FBA includes formal observations of your son and collecting data about his behaviors. In particular, the observer should be recording what happens just before the behaviors (antecedents), and what happens right after the behaviors (consequences). Time and frequency of behaviors should be noted. If some behaviors are accidental, this should be recorded during the observations and the school should try to figure out how to reduce or prevent students and teachers from getting hurt. (As your child has sensory integration disorder, it may be that the occupational therapist needs to consult with the teachers to give them ideas about how to help your child meet his sensory needs in appropriate ways throughout the school day. You also maybe consider looking at diet – especially hidden sugars and screen time.)

The FBA will be used to write a behavior support plan (usually BSP, BP, BIP, etc). This plan describes the behaviors and what, after investigation through taking data, the team believes causes them. Next, it describes what the adults will do to prevent the old behaviors from occurring and replace them with new behaviors, and how adults will react when both old and newly-taught behaviors occur. The focus should be on teaching your son appropriate behaviors and not on punishing him. It should include information about how, and how often, data will be taken, so that progress can be measured.

Tell the school that you wish to be actively involved with developing both the Functional Behavior Assessment and the Behavior Support Plan. If you have information from outside sources that would be helpful, and which you are comfortable sharing it, you should give it to the school when you request the FBA.

It should be easier to problem solve in meetings once there is a Behavior Support Plan in place. Then if the principal insists on reading the list, politely stop him or her, and problem solve each behavior using the information in the assessment and behavior plans. Ask the teachers and therapists what they think may have caused the most recent behavior, exactly what they are doing to teach your child in order to prevent or replace the behavior, and how adults are reacting to the outcomes. (The most important reason to ask this is so that adults are reacting the same way both at home and at school.) If you focus on the behavior plan and problem solving, it will be too time consuming for the principal to read a list of every behavior, and he/she may be reluctant to use the list strategy again. You may want to take a family member, a friend, or an advocate to your meetings who can take notes and share ideas.

23. My child gets very over-stimulated with unstructured activities. Recess is a night-mare and despite 1:1 adult supervision, he does dangerous things. When he gets back into class, he is so "high," he can't get calm enough to sit or attend to instruction, and he is distracting the other kids. What can the school do to help him?

This is a common situation, especially with children as young as your son. Without structure, some children begin to seek ever more intense move-ments, some of which are quite risky. Recess is an important time during the day for all children, both for learning how to interact socially and for the generally positive effects of motor activities on language and learn-ing. In the course of finding a solution to the problem, the first thing to remember is that taking recess away from your child is likely to do more harm than good. It is important to make sure that your child is supervised at recess to stop any very risky activities and make sure he is safe.

It is important to build some calming activities into his school day. One activity that often helps calm children with this type of issue is to per-form some sort of "heavy work," like moving chairs or carrying a stack of books. In addition, sucking or chewing on something helps many children to calm. Florescent lighting can also very stimulating for some children; perhaps the teacher can utilize another type of lighting directly following recess activities and see if this makes a difference for your child.

It sounds like it would be beneficial to find out how your child processes sensory input. Ask your child's teacher and/or the special education teach-er how to arrange an in-school occupational therapy evaluation for sensory processing, or a reevaluation if he has already been evaluated. Put your request in writing, although if this is his only issue, you may be denied this one evaluation.

Ideally, the evaluator will be able to make useful recommendations that can then be used to create a plan for your child and the staff. As this is clearly impacting your child's education (along with the education of his class-mates), and is also a safety issue, this should be a concern for the school as well as you. You might also want to seek a private evaluation with an occupational therapist to get further information, especially if the school does not evaluate him.

24. What do I do next if my child has an IEP in place and he refuses to go to his middle school classes?

I suggest that you request, in writing, an IEP review meeting with the special education team as soon as possible. You should discuss your student's needs, and how the placement and services in the IEP are clearly not producing the desired effect. This may be a difficult situation, as some teams blame the child for not complying without delving further into the situation. It is possible that your child is not going to class just to frustrate the adults. However, we often discover that there are other reasons, for example, the child is getting teased or bullied, feeling stupid, or believing the teacher doesn't like him. It may be that he is unable to do the work, which may not be modified appropriately for him. Many children will not admit what is truly going on; hopefully your child will open up either to you or a trusted school adult as it is difficult to work in a vacuum.

The team needs to consider what may be interfering with the student's education and address that by modifying his program accordingly. A proactive approach should be taken and your child should still receive the services listed on the IEP until a decision has been made regarding the behavior and alternative services.

25. What goes into a behavior plan? Can I see a sample plan?

The plan should contain basic information, such as the child's name and age, a list of who helped write the plan, and what data they used. A current baseline on academic performance, such as grade levels for reading and math, is also often helpful. Before writing the plan, the school team should collect data on your child's behaviors. We suggest that you ask the school or district for the format of the plan they will be using, so you can see what type of information it will include and how it will be laid out.

Here is an example of findings from an FBA and a behavior plan:

1. Clear and specific descriptions of the concerning behaviors.
   a. A good description is "biting bottom lip until it bleeds." A bad description is "purposefully injures himself."
2. A hypothesis, or educated guess, based on data taken, which describes why the child is engaging in the behavior.
   a. The data shows that four out of five days, between 10:00 a.m. – 10:20 a.m., during reading, the 8 year old child who has dyslexia, bites his lip until it bleeds, leaves the class, and goes to the nurse. The day he doesn't bleed is the day that the teacher reads aloud to the class. The hypothesis is that he has figured out a way to get out of "reading" aloud because he is afraid the other kids might laugh at him.
3. The specific new behaviors the child will be taught so that he can get the same needs met, but in a more appropriate way.
   a. To use a secret signal set up with his teacher at times when he does not want to read aloud.
   b. To participate in a small reading class with the literacy teacher.
4. The strategies that will be used to teach the new behaviors
   a. Private discussion initiated by teacher to explore discomfort with reading, and to set up a secret signal to avoid reading aloud, or a class-wide "pass on reading aloud" system.
   b. Class activities examining gifts of each child, and sensitivity training.
   c. Research-based reading lessons.
5. How adults will react when the old behavior occurs.
   a. The teacher will silently hand him the "To Nurse" pass. The nurse will, non-judgmentally and with no emotional reaction, stop the bleeding, and the child will return promptly to class.
6. Crisis intervention plan.
   a. If blood is significant, teacher will contact office to send nurse immediately to classroom to escort child.
7. A date when the plan will be reviewed.
   a. One month.
8. Agreement about how progress will be measured.
   a. Our preference is that this be through ongoing data collection, beginning daily.
   b. Teacher will have "Leaves/Doesn't Leave" checklist taped to her own desk and will mark it before lunch. (If reasonable, the child will be taught to keep a list himself.).

One of my favorite resources on school behavior and behavior plans is Leslie Packer's website: *www.schoolbehavior.com*

Another favorite of mine is Tom McIntyre, PhD's site:

www.behavioradvisor.com

Secret W:
Behavior is the biggest issue your kiddo can exhibit in school. No matter what the school tells you, it is very common for a child to hold it together at school and go home and rage at there – because of what happened in school that day. Do not let the school play the old game of: "It must be from faulty parenting."

---

26. My son is 7 years old and has ADHD. His teacher says that she will have to hold him back if he does not start paying attention. I am so frustrated with her calling to tell me this. I know he has these issues, but his teacher believes he is purposely not paying attention. He had the same behavioral problems at a previous school, but the teacher said that he just needed some "one on one." He passed there with flying colors! She said he was a wonderful student! Help please!

This is rather a two part questions. It's about ADHD, but it's also about retention for any number of reasons.

Here are some things to try. If you haven't already done so, talk with some experts and also see if your child's doctor will write a letter stating that your son has ADHD and how this affects him. (Only do this, if your child really seems to have ADD or ADHD – but know you could be looking at other issues, so think about those prior to simply accepting a prescription.) If the ADHD behaviors are getting in the way at school, as you discovered last year, your son probably needs extra help. Last year's teacher was willing to provide this; this year's teacher and this new school may be willing to do so with written documentation from the doctor.

Next, write a list of everything the previous teacher said your son needed to pay attention and to be more successful in school. Do not just write that he needed "one on one" help. Include what specifically the adult did during this "one on one" time which worked for your son; you may need to contact the previous teacher to find this out. The good news is that if your son was a wonderful student in the past, he can be again with the right help.

Find out as much as you can about how decisions to hold kids back in school are made in your state and school district, and also what your rights are as a parent. You can find this out by contacting your school district or state department of education by phone, or, even better, by searching on their websites. We would not suggest you give your name at this point (or call from your personal phone because of caller ID), as we have sometimes seen district employees who are trying to be helpful, contact the school personnel before you are ready.

Once you have all this information, request a meeting with the teacher, the principal or assistant principal, and any other school people who are involved. Ask early in the meeting for someone from the school to take meeting notes, and ask for a copy. In addition, you should always take your own notes, or bring someone with you to do that.

Secret X:
Some time ago, I started to audiotape all of the meetings I went to on a terrific phone app called AudioMemos, as what I've found is that we are all busy and so many times, people just don't remember what they agree to. Even I don't always remember exactly what was said! With the meeting on tape and using my notes, I can quickly go back and find out exactly what people discussed and decided upon. (By the way, why this app? It has some great features, including compressing the file, breaking it into segments, very clear sound, and it's easy to attach to an email.)

Start by thanking the teacher for bringing the concerns to your attention; it is always easier to convince people if they feel they are heard and it was really a good thing for the teacher to let you know early on about the problems. Share the information you have from the previous teacher (in a non-threatening manner) and ask them to try these ideas and collect data on the outcomes. Set a date to meet and reevaluate.

Once moving forward is all taken care of, ask how the decision to hold your son back will be made. This way you will know what to do if the school wants to hold him back and you do not agree, or if you believe they should hold him back (with a new plan for learning) and they don't agree to that. Let them know your thoughts on this at the meeting if you know your response; I imagine you may want to take some time after the meeting to consider this important decision. If you disagree with anything at this meeting, or if you feel the information they gave you about how the decision is made conflicts with what you learned from the district or the state, make sure this is documented by the school in the meeting notes.

Before leaving this meeting, ask to set up another meeting to review all the decisions and agreements, including follow up dates and data to be collected. Be sure to write a polite follow-up letter, summarizing decisions, your concerns, and anything you disagreed with. You may want to find a family member, friend, or advocate who can go with you to the meeting to help take notes, give you moral support, and help speak up for your child and his needs.

I remember a friend calling me up years ago, telling me a lot of the kids in her town were held back before kindergarten so as to give them a better chance both at sports and getting into an ivy league school. She felt her son was ready for kindergarten, but her friends were all pointing out how short he was for his age. She asked what I thought. I pondered for a moment, and then asked what she would do if he didn't grow much the following year, if she would keep him back again. She laughed, enrolled him in kindergarten, and he both played sports well AND went to a top college. (In general, I do think it is best if you are going to hold a child back, to do it before kindergarten, especially with all the demands that exist these days in kindergarten – and especially if your child is already in special education and receiving good programming. Just because a child has a disability should not preclude giving him one more year of growth at the onset of school.)

In recent years, I have been involved with less than a dozen kids where retention came up for a variety of reasons. Sometimes I've supported it and sometimes I have not. It really depends on the child and on the individual circumstances. And very fortunately, I've been incredibly lucky to have been right in each of those situations.

I do think it is a really bad idea to hold a child back and then do exactly the same things (usually nothing special) that were done the year before. That makes no sense at all and is usually a waste of time and leads to feelings of failure. On the other hand, sometimes kids really do need an extra year of elementary school – at the beginning or towards the end. Middle school can be really tough if you are missing the foundations, or if you're really immature. Sometimes intervention simply started too late and it is so much simpler to supply that in an extra year of elementary school. Sometimes, even though needed services should be available at the middle school level, the 5th or 6th grade special ed teacher at the elementary school has exactly the training your child needs. Sometimes you just started your child too early – especially as our schools now force 5 year old boys, who in particular, should be learning by playing, to sit in chairs and do paperwork for hours on demand. These days, a kid really can fail kindergarten!

Note: Retaining a child is a very, very emotional subject for everyone involved. Based on how I have observed responses, I think it must bring up all of our childhood insecurities. I sat in one meeting where we were determining retention for a 5th grader who was severely behind in math and reading because of crummy special education services to address his dyslexia in his early years of school. Earlier that year, his last year in elementary school, I attended the IEP meeting as his advocate and persuaded them not only to use a research-based program suited for his disabilities, but also to do it as prescribed for 90 minutes a day, 5 days a week. He made so much progress in reading that year, but was still far behind and still pretty lost in math and writing. The child himself wanted to stay back one more year to catch up. The special ed coordinator shared how her husband was still hurt and angry that he himself had been retained at one point, and she cautioned against retaining the boy. And then the child's mother jumped in, explaining that her brother, the child's uncle, had also been retained, and was now a judge who believes had he not been retained, it would likely have impacted his success. She said that in their family, it's a plus to be retained.

Generally, if you are looking at retention, consider switching schools to minimize teasing by other kids. That's really important. And don't decide on the basis of whether or not your kid will throw your decision in your face in teenage years. Having raised adolescents and survived, I truly believe that no matter what you decide about pretty much anything, you will be told you were wrong, that you understand nothing, and that you are the worst parent in the world. Just make your best decision.

In any case, it is important to know that schools can give extra help in a variety of ways. If your child is not progressing because of his inattention or other issues, he may be able to get help through general education. If your child's needs are intensifying, and he does not already have these services, he may need special education support now, or in the future. Having a letter from the doctor will help if that is the path to follow. The school will need to evaluate him, and the team (including you) will decide if he is eligible for special education services. If the school is threatening to hold him back, clearly the ADHD is affecting his education. If your child needs "one on one" help, and if you cannot get it, or enough of it from the school, you may want to plan extra time to work with your child yourself, and/or engage a tutor. Remember, schools don't provide everything your child needs to succeed. If your child is already receiving special education services, he may need more of them, or a different type of help. The school can also provide extra assistance through RTI or provide accommodations through a 504.

Sign Up Here For Your Free Gift
Be sure to sign up right now for the free video series by going to www.getieptips.com . The tips address the answers to the most common how-to questions about the results you are seeking when it comes to your child learning. There are twenty-one 2 - 3 minute videos included.

Chapter Six: Placement

It's About My Child.
What Makes Them So Right?

Hi Yael, Need you to get involved. They want to put my child in a new placement and I absolutely don't agree with moving him. Please call me.

Hi Yael, Need you to get involved. My child is not learning anything in this placement – how do we get a new one? Oh, and by the way, what does it mean that a placement isn't necessarily a place? Please call me back.

Secret Y:
A "PLACEMENT" is not necessarily a place.
This is important!

First, many parents are surprised to find out that the "placement" is not necessarily a "place." It is actually a description of the type of programming, the number of hours of programming, the type of support necessary to effectively teach a child, and the amount of time a child will be educated with typical peers. Where the programming will be provided is a "location," and will not necessarily be described or included in the "placement;" you may have to negotiate a school preference separately. I have been at many meetings during which a set number of hours is offered based on what the school or the district usually allots for a certain age or disability type; such decisions should instead be based on the needs of the individual child.

Next, principals are powerful figures. They are responsible for the education and safety of all students in the school, and can be quite unyielding and vocal in their efforts to ensure this. While principals have a duty to respond if they see your child's behavior as a potential risk to others, they do not have the authority to change your child's placement on their own. There are many options that should be explored before your child's placement is changed and then, any decision to change a placement is made by the IEP team.

For whatever reason, if your child's behavior is a significant issue and is preventing him from receiving an education or disrupting the school enenvironment for other students, it's essential that you talk with the school about how to address this. You will want to request, in writing, that the school perform a Functional Behavior Assessment for your child, and then create a Behavior Support Plan. Please see the answers to Questions 22 and 25 for more information about this. It may also be important to conduct other evaluations, explore your child's strengths and needs more fully, and review the IEP, including looking at additional services your child may need in order to be more successful in school.

As always, remember that it is important to take notes at meetings and keep copies of any written communication from the principal that indicate that he or she wants your child to go to a different school or placement. (I'd for sure be recording these meetings – let the school know you are.) Each time the principal indicates this, ask what other options are being considered before suggesting a placement change, and record the answer.

Changing schools can be very disruptive for any child, so it is likely that you will want to avoid this scenario if possible, unless you really believe that your child should make that change. There can be excellent reasons for making a change, and you should also consider those in making your decision. It is essential that you take a family member, a friend, or an advocate to every meeting to help take notes, supply moral support, and add information about your child.

28. What if the school district suggests the most restrictive environment for my child and I disagree? What is the process?

When the IEP team decides upon placement for the student, it may be that the school-based members of the IEP team recommend a placement with, which you disagree. It is very important to make sure you fully understand why the team feels your child's IEP cannot be implemented in a less restrictive environment and to ask for Prior Written Notice, which means that they must put their reasoning in writing. It is also important that you review your child's IEP very closely and are sure you understand it.

It does not matter what the basis of the placement disagreement is (in some situations, parents want a more restrictive setting than the school-based members of the team recommend), because the process is the same. You must communicate, in writing, saying you disagree with a change in placement for your child. You should also voice this at the IEP meeting during which placement is discussed. I strongly suggest that you refrain from announcing that you are going to sue the school or take them to due process without consulting an attorney who specializes in special education law, as there are rules and time limits that must be followed. It could be advisable to call for another IEP meeting and ask an advocate or attorney to attend. Sometimes an advocate can work out an agreement without involving further legal remedies, and sometimes you do need an attorney.

Secret Z:
No matter how angry you get, don't threaten due process at a meeting – unless you have already spoken to a special education attorney and you have planned this! Watch your tone if you do say it.

If you and the rest of the team cannot come to an agreement, then you may utilize mediation or a due process hearing in order to determine placement for your child. Mediation does not cost the parents anything except time (and perhaps for an advocate). It is designed to assist the parents and school district to reach a mutually acceptable agreement, which will then be binding. The mediator will explain the process to you. Due process is time consuming, complicated, emotionally draining, and expensive as it involves attorney's and expert witness' fees. It's an important tool, **BUT SHOULD NOT** be the first and only one in your toolbox. Unless the placement change is for disciplinary reasons, the child's current placement must be maintained until the due process hearing is completed and placement is decided by the hearing officer (who, of course, does not know your child).

It is not appropriate for the school team to recommend a substantial placement change unless they have conducted evaluations to determine the child's needs. As a parent, you can disagree with the school's evaluations and request an independent educational evaluation (IEE) at the expense of the school district prior to the change in placement. As always, you need to do this in writing. According to the rules, you are not required (and don't need to explain) why you disagree with the evaluations. Be very brief. The school district can agree to pay for the evaluations and may provide you with criteria for the evaluations. If the district says yes, and asks you to sign communication releases with the evaluators, I usually suggest you write in that your permission is given with the restriction that you are to simultaneously receive any test scores and reports that the school district receives from the evaluator, and that you will be present in any and all discussions they have with evaluators. If the district says no, you will either need to give in, or request mediation or due process. Again, if you are considering a legal response, you should first consult an advocate or attorney. Mediation (see Question 8) is often preferable to jumping into a due process; it's much less stressful and much less expensive.

Technically, you are able to go out and get an IEE on your own and then present the bill to the school district. Although there certainly can be good reasons to get an IEE without informing the school district in advance, there is no guarantee that they will pay for it, especially without a fight. I've found that the most crucial piece is to get a highly qualified evaluator(s) for the evaluation.

Two of my favorite resources on this topic are advocate Judy Bonnell's article "How To Use a Parent Attachment" which can be found at *www.wrightslaw.com/advoc/tips/Judy_IEP_Attachment.html* along with Attorney Sonja Kerr's article, "How to Handle Disagreements at IEP Meetings (or Playing 20 Questions with the Devil)" which you can find at *www.wrightslaw.com/advoc/guest/Kerr_Meetings_Progess.htm*

Sonja Kerr, Esq. advises to create a form to use at the IEP meeting, with three columns labeled "What Mom Wants," "School's Response," and "Resolved?" She writes that "the worst thing that can occur is that you note that the school has not responded and nothing is resolved" but, "the best thing that happens is that they actually respond to you and you know where you stand. If they don't respond, this shows that the school is not listening to you. This forms the basis for your position that you are not an equal participant in the IEP process and that your child is being denied FAPE (a Free Appropriate Public Education)."

29. Last month, my son got an IEP for a learning disability in reading and writing. His school is now saying that they may have been mistaken and that he didn't qualify for help in reading and writing. They said they may have to take one of his services back. Can a school take back an IEP after it's signed and agreed upon? I thought that it was a legally binding contract.

If the school continues to say they have to remove services, request (in writing) that they put their decision to withdraw services and their reasons for doing so in writing. In the same letter, ask that they provide you with the state guidelines about eligibility for special education services for children with learning disabilities, or go to your state department of education website and look for the guidelines there. Take a close look at all the information you get and write a list of questions you want the school team to answer. You may want to contact an advocate to help you review this information and write the list of questions.

Finally, request an IEP team meeting so you can ask your questions. Take a family member, friend, or advocate to the meeting with you. It may be that the school is correct in their reasoning, or that you can get them to continue the services he needs. If they are suggesting that your child should no longer have an IEP, you might also find that your child qualifies for services under RTI or a 504 Plan. Bring this up with the IEP team. I'd definitely get at least a consult on something like this and likely have the district pay for an independent evaluation. People can make mistakes.

Sign Up Here For Your Free Gift
Be sure to sign up right now for the free video series by going to www.getieptips.com . The tips address the answers to the most common how-to questions about the results you are seeking when it comes to your child learning. There are twenty-one 2 - 3 minute videos included.

Chapter Seven: Autism

1 in 45, But Your Child Is Not Just a Statistic

 Hello, Yael? My child is diagnosed with autism, and the school district says that the best way for him to make progress is to learn by osmosis. Ok, that's not the word they used, but it's the same thing. The only way he has ever learned anything is by ABA, and that's not their plan. His team said he should go into one of their autism programs. I went to observe and he would get only 20 minutes of instructional time from the teacher a day. The rest of the time, the kids are just stimming. There's a really good private program, but they said they won't send him there, because they say they can provide this – but I know it's really about the money. Please call me.

Secret AA:
Yup, it's the law, but it really is about the money. That's really not a secret. ABA is scientifically-based excellent teaching. It's almost always about the money.

---

30. The IEP team has told me that I should let the school test for autism because if my child is on the spectrum, she will get more services. Is this true?

It is NOT correct that an educational identification of an autism spectrum disorder will guarantee more services for your daughter. One child on the spectrum may look very different than another child with the same diagnosis. The type and amount of special education services your daughter gets should depend upon a full evaluation of her strengths and needs. These evaluations could include testing which looks at skills typically affected in kids who are on the spectrum, but it should include a variety of other tests and in-school observations.

Secret BB
Don't get legal information from the school district.
You must always get this double-checked.
Sure, sometimes people who know better will tell you
something that's not so, but most of the teachers and
therapists are not so well-versed in the law and
they may really believe what they are telling you is true.

---

31. What do you do when you disagree with the school district's placement for your 3 yr old who has autism?

This is really a two-part question.

The first question is what you do when you disagree with any placement that the IEP team is making. For that answer, see Question 28.

With autism, the real question to ask is: In light of the research on early intervention and autism, what type of placement is really appropriate for a young child?

To answer, let's start with a comparison. You have your child tested and discover he has a specific type of leukemia. You check on the internet and discover that, thanks to research, this disease can be treated with success rates of approximately 80% survival with a good quality of life. What would you do if your doctor then said, "Oh, no, I think we'll try this other standard treatment that we used to use (with much lower survival rates), and we'll get back together to evaluate in a year," or "The research-based treatment is to administer this drug once a day for four months, but we decided we'll give it to your child just once a week for three months because that is the amount of time we give medication to children with other diseases." Well, I imagine you'd change doctors. It's no different with autism; there is scientific research about how to treat children with autism and it is called "Applied Behavior Analysis (ABA)." This is what you want to seek.

Despite the research, it is not always easy to get ABA services from many school districts. In fact, unless your district is one of those that already uses Applied Behavior Analysis as the framework, it can be quite complicated. I recommend you seek assistance in attempting to do so. There are many children in the country who do receive ABA therapy (home-based or school-based) from the school district. You may need to use a joint approach towards funding a total program for your child; the school is only one piece of this very intensive programming which usually involves 25 – 60 hours of therapy a week. In some states, insurance companies have mandated that insurance pays at least a portion of this service. I believe it is crucial that, as parents of a child with autism, you educate yourself about ABA, as you will need to be involved. See the links below to begin.

What is ABA for autism? In brief, it is the framework surrounding the therapies and methodologies used, that include breaking down skills into small pieces (task analysis), teaching the skills in small steps using error-less learning (See *www.projectlearnet.org/tutorials/errorless_learning.html*), heavily reinforcing correct responses, repeating until mastery, taking data, and analyzing the data scientifically to plan the next steps. It may or may not include "discrete teaching" or pieces from other methodologies; that will depend on the particular child and the analysis of the data.

According to the experts:

> *"Thirty years of research demonstrated the efficacy of applied behavioral methods in reducing inappropriate behavior and in increasing communication, learning, and appropriate social behavior."* Satcher, D. (1999). Mental health: A report of the surgeon general. U.S. Public Health Service. Bethesda, MD.

> *"Over 30 years of rigorous research and peer review of applied behavior analysis' effectiveness for individuals with autism demonstrate ABA has been objectively substantiated as effective based upon the scope and quality of science."* Maine Administrators of Services for Children with Disabilities (2000). Report of the MADSEC Autism Task Force. MADSEC, Manchester, ME.

> *"Based upon strong scientific evidence, it is recommended that principles of applied behavior analysis and behavior intervention strategies be included as an important element of any intervention program for young children with autism."* New York State Department of Health Early Intervention Program. (1999). Clinical Practice Guideline Report of the Recommendations for Autism/Pervasive Developmental Disorders. New York State Department of Health, Albany, NY.

32. My son who has PDD (Pervasive Developmental Disorder, which is on the autism spectrum), is in a full day preschool disability program with his own aide. He receives both speech and OT. With district funding, he also attends a private preschool with the same aide. The district has just evaluated him with standardized tests and found him to be "average." Now the district wants to place him in a regular Kindergarten with no special services in the fall. Can they really not offer him specialized services and boot him out of special education on the basis of tests, without looking at his functional performance?

Formal tests are only a part of the picture when it comes to deciding if a child is eligible for special education services, especially as formal tests are given by predictable adults in a one-to-one quiet environment. Observations from teachers about performance are also important. This is especially so for a child as young as your son, because very few formal evaluation tools can be used with such young children. It may also be that some further formal testing needs to be performed to look at behavioral and social functioning in the classroom. The school district must evaluate your child in all the areas that his disability impacts him. If you believe the district has omitted a major area, then you can request that they evaluate it.

If the teachers in the current preschool settings have observed the difficulties, you can ask that they submit a report to the IEP team (and attend an IEP meeting which you should request in writing). The IEP team must take this information into consideration when deciding placement for Kindergarten. You can also request a private evaluation at school district expense, which the district will have to consider – once they do their evaluation. See Question 28 for information about requesting independent educational evaluations.

If you ask for a review of your child's placement and the school district refuses, you can request mediation from your state department of education. Mediation is voluntary and the district does not have to agree to mediate. If they refuse, your recourse at that point may be to seek out an advocate or an attorney. See Question 8 for more information.

33. My seven year old son has autism and lots of issues. He isn't potty trained and can't feed himself. He has very few things he will eat, and will only eat them if an adult feeds him. The school told me that they believe he can physically feed himself, so they won't do it for him. They said that if they do feed him, he won't become independent. My son is not eating or drinking at school because of this. What can I do about the situation in school? Is there any research on how to support kids with autism to learn to eat independently?

Start with getting a letter from your son's pediatrician stating what his food intake has to be at lunchtime. The letter also needs to say that, if necessary, your child must be fed by an adult to ensure eating. Give a copy of the letter to the school and ask them to write a health plan that includes all the information from the doctor. Ask for the involvement of the school nurse in writing the health plan and implementing it. This should take care of the school lunch problem.

Secret CC:
When you have a problem that involves your child's health, get the school/district nurse involved. They have nursing licenses and abide by ethics, not funding.

Next, some of my contacts (both professionals and experienced parents) came up with several suggestions for you:

First, take a look at a book called *Baby Bites: Transforming a Picky Eater into a Healthy Eater* by Nonna Joann Bruso. Her methods, useful for many children, have been used successfully with some children who have eating issues as part of their autism.

Next, explore Judy Converse's website: *www.nutritioncare.net*. Judy Converse is a licensed, registered dietician specializing in children with autism. She has several published books, with one called: *Your Child's Special Diet: Strategies to Help Children With Autism Learn, Grow, and Thrive.*

Finally, if all else fails and you are desperate, here is the advice of a dad of one of my clients with autism who had severe feeding issues:

If you want results, contact Dr. Tom Linscheid at Ohio State University (OSU) Children's Hospital, now called Nationwide Children's Hospital, where we went; our son's progress was amazing and he eats regular food now. We met another family who had a similar issue with their six year old child who was on the autism spectrum and was also failing to thrive. He had "mild" autism, but he just could not "do eating." I shared with them what we had done with our child and they thought it was extreme. Our child was much more "involved," and the mother had no reason to think that there was any similarity between my son and hers. Almost a year and a half later, we met again, and the mother fell around my neck, sobbing, and exhausted. They had just come back from

OSU, and their child was eating! That was a year ago, and the child is doing fine, still eating. I am convinced that Dr. Linscheid's clinic is the only solution for families who have tried everything for children such as ours.

Sign Up Here For Your Free Gift

Be sure to sign up right now for the free video series by going to www.getieptips.com . The tips address the answers to the most common how-to questions about the results you are seeking when it comes to your child learning. There are twenty-one 2 - 3 minute videos included.

Chapter Eight: Curriculum & Methodology

Are We Singing From Different Hymnals?

Hi Yael, My 3rd grader is just not learning; could it be the curriculum? The class size? The methodologies? The teaching style? Please give me a call back.

34. If a child does not qualify for special education, can a special education teacher tell a regular classroom teacher to modify work for her?

In some situations, children are found not eligible for special education services, but the team feels that some extra interventions would be helpful. Although these interventions are the responsibility of the regular education team including teachers and literacy specialists, schools can also use special education staff to support kids who are not making adequate progress. Each state defines for itself what adequate progress is, sets targets for progress, and tests students each year to see if progress is being made.

As we have explained previously, if you are being told that your daughter is not eligible for special education services, the first step is to fully understand the results of the evaluations and the criteria for eligibility. If you disagree with the evaluations, you can request an independent educational evaluation. If you disagree with the decision about eligibility, you can request mediation. If the school has informed you that she is not eligible for testing, put your request in writing. No one should determine whether a child will meet the criteria for special education without an evaluation.

In addition, you can ask what interventions the school can provide to your daughter, using regular education or special education resources, to ensure adequate progress. You will have some idea if these interventions are working when you receive her report cards, the results of any state testing, school achievement testing, in addition to her work samples and comments about how she is doing in school. Please remember that schools do not do everything; you may need to engage a tutor to help your daughter succeed.

If your daughter's work is already being modified, this does suggest that she may need some extra support at school. Ask the teachers to put in writing exactly what modifications they are recommending and why. There is a difference between modifications and accommodations. Modifications require someone to review the curriculum and make changes to content, but accommodations include such items as seating your child near the teacher, letting her use a calculator, or allowing her to use a special pencil grip for writing, while the curriculum expectations remain the same.

35. My middle school daughter needs one on one instruction if she is to learn to read. The school has her in a small group of kids with mixed abilities, most of whom are also nonreaders. I observed a session last week, and the teacher was instructing them about making sentences, and asked the kids to list some nouns and verbs. I know my child has no clue what these are. On other days, they are doing something called "Balanced Reading." Why are they teaching her things she is not ready to learn, and not teaching her how to read? What should I ask them to do?

You are so right to be concerned about your child's reading ability. Reading is a crucial life skill. The National Re ading Panel guidelines stress that reading instruction should be based on scientific research. Here are the areas of reading instruction that they   concluded any good program should include:

PHONEMIC AWARENESS (the ability to focus on and manipulate the smallest sounds in spoken words; the word "go" has two phonemes "g" and "o".)

EXPLICIT AND SYSTEMATIC PHONICS INSTRUCTION (how let-ters correspond to sounds and how to use this knowledge in reading and spelling)

READING FLUENCY (guided repeated oral reading has a significant and positive impact on word recognition, reading fluency, and comprehen-sion for students of all ages)

VOCABULARY, and

READING COMPREHENSION

One of my favorite resources for information about reading instruction of young children is *www.readingrockets.org*. It contains a multitude of articles, webcasts, and other resources. It contains a special section called "Helping Struggling Readers," which I recommend you read.

It is important that schools use a research-based methodology to teach reading. Sometimes, only children with a diagnosed learning disabili-ty receive this type of methodology; sometimes even they receive only more of the same thing that is already not working. It is also important that parents follow through with making sure their children learn to read no matter what the school does. Taking your child to a tutor, a reading clinic, or a specialized school that uses a research-based reading program is one answer, if funds allow. If finances are an issue, read the Read-ing Rocket's article on "Breaking Barriers Without Breaking the Bank" *www.readingrockets.org/article/breaking-barriers-without-breaking-bank* for other ideas to get your daughter the help she needs, sooner rather than later.

Secret DD:
You really need a research-based reading program for your child, especially if your child is dyslexic. Not just any reading program will do! And, if the school has been doing a research-based reading program for dyslexic kids, and it is not working – you need to check on what the program says the correct amount per day is, if they are following the program instructions, etc. That's just as crucial.

---

36. Have there been any studies on whether children in the early grades with ADHD, sensory integration issues, etc., are more successful in school if they do or don't have homework? My child and I end up totally stressed over homework every night!

There have been several studies on the effects of homework on children with disabilities in the early grades. It has been determined that it is not the quantity of homework, but the quality that is derived from the homework that is most important. If a child has an IEP, it should be stated within the accommodations and modifications section of the IEP how homework will be given, and the amount of time and effort that a child will need to focus on homework. Hopefully, parents will be able to adjust the amount when it's an overload; many teachers allow that.

There are many findings that negate the benefits of homework alto-gether, whether the student is in regular education or special education. Homework often causes loss of interest in learning, impacts the re-lationships of parents and children, as well the relationships of all the members in the household. Studies have shown little or no academic benefit from assigning homework in elementary or middle school. Al-fie Cohen has written a book called *The Homework Myth: Why Our Kids Get Too Much of a Bad Thing*. You can read his summarizing article about the research, his findings, and his suggestions for parents and children at *www.alfiekohn.org/articles.htm#null* and clicking *Rethinking Homework*. Anoth-er book, *The Case Against Homework*, by Bennett and Kalish, examines the research in the U.S. and around the world.

The fact is that most children will receive homework, and there are teach-ers who certainly feel that homework is important. If a child with ADD, or any other learning challenge, is getting homework, here are some things parents and teachers need to consider:

- the child's strengths and needs

- how the child learns

- what the adults are hoping the child will gain from homework assign-ments

- how the child best demonstrates knowledge and skills

- how any given homework assignment fits into this picture, so that it can be modified as necessary for this child.

For good articles on how to communicate, organize, and strategize to make homework more efficient and calmer, read *Homework Practices that Support Students With Disabilities* at: *peakparent.org/pdf/fact_sheets/homework.pdf.*

37. I have an unmotivated and inconsistent 16 year old with developmental disabilities. I have found some things to motivate her when using discrete trial teaching with flashcards, but she burns out on them fast, even if I make sure to mix them up. She does better with real-life situations than with cards. Are there other ways to do discrete trial without using flashcards?

It sounds like the roadblock may not just be motivation, but about making the learning more meaningful for your daughter too, especially as a teenager. Discrete trial training, while important for building particular skills, does not usually generalize without being blended with other enjoyable activities in a variety of places. As your daughter may be a bit of a concrete thinker in the way she learns, she may need to see it, feel it, do it, and learn how it fits into her life in a useful way, because it gets her a natural reward for her efforts.

So, when she is learning math, it may be more meaningful if she is earning allowance for chores, or using her allowance to buy something she enjoys, rather than having her do a math activity using flash cards. If reading is a goal, find something your daughter needs to read in order to get something she enjoys. For example, if she has favorite meals, get her to choose them from a list of recipe cards. Make sure to reward her by making it for dinner that day, so check your cupboards for ingredients before you offer a choice! Your daughter could work on even more skills if she is prepared to help make the meal! If your daughter is not yet reading, pair a written list with pictures. (Attainment Company has some nice resources for this.)

Spend some time listing the skills you want your daughter to gain, and break them down into the tiny pieces she will need to master to achieve each skill. Put the list of skills in order, first, second, etc., and check off the ones your daughter already has. You will then have an organized checklist of discrete skills to teach your daughter. Often, people start teaching the skills closest to the end of the list, because then there is no delay in getting the reward for a job well done. This increases motivation and helps build some momentum. Then, you just keep working backwards, linking the skills together until you reach the start. Make a list of all the real life activities your daughter enjoys, which provide opportunities to teach the skills you have listed. Always keep the focus on the reward and not the task. For more information and examples of task analysis, go to *www.behavioradvisor.com.*

You also might want to check out the following resources about older children: *www.researchautism.org/resources/reading/index.asp* and *verbalbehavior.pbwiki.com/ABA+for+those+5+and+older*

38. I would like the best possible education for my son who has Down Syndrome (or any other disability). What should I look for in a school?

Talk to other parents and contact your local Down Syndrome associations for recommendations. When you have a list of schools, look at their brochures or websites. Ask yourself, "Do their values and mission statements sound like my own? Do they have the types and amounts of support I think are necessary to meet my son's special education needs?"

Ideally, you are looking for a school in which your son will be included with typical kiddos, but which is also able to teach your child at his own pace and style of learning. Arrange to visit any school, including your neighborhood school, that interests you, and try to arrange a brief meeting with the principal and someone from the special education team. Take a list of your child's strengths, needs, and interests to the visit, and ask the school what they can offer that would be a match with this list.

You want a school that has high standards for your child, along with expectations that your child will learn to read, do math, and cover the same academic areas as all kids. Ask the school about which teaching strategies they think might be appropriate for your son. They should be able to share some ideas; if this question is met with silence, you may have a problem. The school should also expect that your son will make friends and take part in the same after school activities as other kids; ask how they can help with this.

Secret EE:
One very important thing to remember is that you cannot talk about "best" in the IEP meeting in a public school, as all that is required is an "appropriate" education.* The analogy that is often used is that you are not entitled to a Cadillac, only to a Chevy. Of course, to that, your response should be that your child will still need the gas (good teaching and good methods) to power the Chevy. *In the 10th Circuit, thanks to the Elizabeth E special education case, the standard is "meaningful" education.

And finally, you are looking for a group of professionals with whom you think you will be able to plan and problem solve. They need to be able to listen to you (and you to them) and be willing to act on your expertise as a parent. If they disagree with you, they need to be able to say so respectfully and with honesty, but be willing to compromise. Remember there are no perfect schools, but look for the best match. Then, use your intuition.

Sign Up Here For Your Free Gift
Be sure to sign up right now for the free video series by going to www.getieptips.com . The tips address the answers to the most common how-to questions about the results you are seeking when it comes to your child learning. There are twenty-one 2 - 3 minute videos included.

Chapter Nine: Help Wanted

She Doesn't Have To Fall, Or Fail

Hi Yael, My child has a seizure disorder and she falls down often. The school district says that it's not bad enough to give her a 1:1 aide. They're also planning on putting her into a program that is a half hour away from our home, including a steep mountain ride. I'd rather she go to our neighborhood school. Can you make this happen? Please call me.

39. My child has severe epilepsy with the kind of seizures that cause her to fall down. This happens each day. I would like to have an aide accompany my child on the school bus.

I suggest you visit your child's physician and discuss the issue. Ask the doctor to write a letter stating that your child needs supervision during the bus journey, due to the frequency of seizures, along with the potential health and safety concerns should a seizure happen on the bus. Then, in writing, request an "IEP Review" meeting to discuss health and safety issues that are impacting your daughter's education. Mention in your written request that a school or district nurse should be invited to the meeting; follow up on this by making a phone call to the nurse to make sure she is invited.

At the meeting, share the doctor's letter and ask the school to write a health plan which outlines the supports your child needs during and after a seizure, along with any pro-active steps the school needs to take in order to reduce the risk of injury caused by a fall. At this point, request an aide on the bus be included in the Health Plan and IEP.

If the team does not agree to an aide, ask them to include in the meeting notes that you have requested a bus aide to keep your daughter from getting hurt. Most districts supply 1:1 aides for safety concerns.

After the meeting, write a letter to the Special Education Director and the Superintendent, describing the situation, and ask them to explain why you were turned down for an aide on the bus for your daughter since this is a safety issue. If you don't have success this way, consider going to the Board of Education. Generally Boards of Education have a public input time and each person is allotted 2-3 minutes to speak on any subject connected to education. Depending on the Board's rules, you can combine time with someone else. Call the Superintendent's office in your district to find out how it works in your district. Parents I know have had a fair amount of success going to the Board of Education when nothing else works; usually the President of the Board looks over at the Superintendent and says, "You'll take care of this, right?"

40. How do I get an aide for my daughter at school?

Start by gathering as much information as you can. Review all the documentation, such as your daughter's IEP and any private evaluations you have, and then talk with the teachers, so that you are able to clearly explain why she needs an aide. Once you have identified your daughter's needs, work with the team to identify strategies for meeting those needs; using an aide is one possibility. On one hand, an aide can be a wonderful and essential resource for your child, but an aide can also be a barrier to peer interaction, as other kids may avoid your daughter if she is generally accompanied by an adult, especially one who may not be skilled in facilitating friendships. Of course, if you can get both, your daughter will likely be better off.

Where possible, you want to focus on getting the school to teach your child the skills she needs to become as independent as she can, as an alternative to relying on another person. On the other hand, you do not want to trade independence for learning.

In many districts, aides are often only provided to kids who have health and/or safety needs, such as a medical condition or behavioral issues. If your child has a medical condition, a letter from the doctor stating that supervision is needed for health reasons may help. If your child has behavioral issues, ask the school to collect data about the behaviors and to consider supporting your child with an aide. Once you have collected the information, ask for a meeting to review it all and request an aide both verbally and in writing. If the school/district does not agree, they will also need to respond in writing to your request and explain why. If your child needs an aide to learn or to be safe, don't give up. Politely continue to press your case and keep good records, so that you can support the need for an aide. You may need an attorney.

41. My son is in 10th grade and is failing. I feel the school district is not helping. I've called the learning support teacher several times, with no response. What are my rights and how can I get help?

What you need is a meeting to discuss your son's needs. Request it by writing to the learning support teacher with copies to his regular education teachers as well as the principal. The school should respond promptly to your written meeting request. If you then feel that the school is still not responsive, contact the special education director, the district administrator for secondary education, or the superintendent's office by phone with a follow up letter. You may want to invite the special education director for secondary schools to the meeting.

Secret FF:
Put it in writing. Putting requests in writing has a
much better chance of getting something to happen!

---

42. My son who is in middle school is not able to take notes, and also needs emotional support. He would like me to be in all his classes with him, and I am available to do this. It would allow me to reinforce what is taught in class, as well as take notes. The school says that because he is mainstreamed and fully included, he has what is called a "shadow aide," who is a person who comes in for only about 20 minutes in the middle of the class, because he also has to go help students in other classrooms. What difference does it really make to anyone if I were to give my child the emotional support of knowing I am in the back of the classroom? I would not interfere with teaching. I would simply take notes for my son to use later for homework and studying.

This is definitely a very difficult and sensitive situation that you will be placing yourself and your child into. Middle school and high school can be cruel settings for kids who are trying to socialize and become a part of the mainstream crowd. I suggest that if your child is unable to take notes in the classroom, you speak to the special education teacher or the 504 representative for the school (or district), and ensure your son has accommodations for a scribe. The other possible option is to request that your son get copies of notes, taken either by the teacher or by other students who take accurate, legible notes in class. This lets your child simply concentrate on the class and not feel overwhelmed by the need to take notes Notetaker services are usually provided to students that have difficulty hearing, reading, or writing, or teacher notes can be made available. While I understand your desire to have your child be successful in the school setting, with an authorized notetaker in the class, teachers and students will likely be more accepting of the situation and your son..

Another valuable resource is a Livescribe pen which syncs voice with writing and drawing. It will allow you to go over material with your son later in the day.

If you suspect your child is getting bullied, and that is part of the issue, first talk with your child, and if this is so, call immediately for a special education meeting to discuss meeting his emotional needs.

43. Can I ask for vision therapy to be added to my child's IEP? Since all the testing from the school mentions "visual perception problems," I feel this would benefit him greatly.

Contacting some of our nationwide resources, we discovered that Vision Therapy (VT) is indeed provided for children with IEP's in some states. It seems that the parents who are successful in getting this service are "persistent" advocates. However, some school districts believe VT to be controversial and will not pay for the service regardless of how well the parent advocates, or how often school people mention visual problems. Keep good records and put everything in writing. It's certainly worth a try.

44. Is professional development for paraeducators a federal mandate?

There has been growing concern for a long time to have trained paraeducators, especially for those who provide instruction to students. Most states have certification and licensing in addition to training. In particular, states want to ensure staff members are adequately trained to provide special education and related services. Note, however, that this can range from having a GED to college education. Check your state and school district requirements for more information. Also, make sure you understand exactly what is appropriate for a paraeducator to do as opposed to a licensed teacher. It's fine for most paraeducators to review, to help supervise, to help kids stay on task. Frankly, I prefer that instruction be given by a trained teacher. When you request a paraeducator, you are likely to get one without a teaching license to teach your child in the place of a highly qualified teacher. In that case, you will want to push either for a highly qualified teacher, or at least training for the paraeducator and limits to what that person is allowed to do when it comes to instruction.

Special Education paraeducators work under the supervision of the special education teacher. On-the-job training usually takes place during the work day. If you believe that further training would be helpful, you could discuss this with the special education teacher, the principal, or the district administration.

Secret GG:
If you would like to read a more in-depth report
regarding special education teachers
and paraeducators, go to
www.parentcenterhub.org/repository/paras/ **which is the new**
website for the articles and resources that were
previously on The National Information Center for
Children and Youth with Disabilities (NICHCY).

Sign Up Here For Your Free Gift
Be sure to sign up right now for the free video
series by going to www.getieptips.com . The tips
address the answers to the most common how-to
questions about the results you are seeking when
it comes to your child learning. There are
twenty-one 2 - 3 minute videos included.

Chapter Ten: Evaluations

Don't You Want To Help?

 **Hi Yael, I've got a problem. I think my child should be tested for Special Ed. I've asked everyone there to test him, but even the office secretary told me that they won't test him because he's too smart. He may be smart, but he struggles. What do I do? Can they really deny him this?**

45. Will the testing team at the school tell me everything I need to know about what my daughter needs?

Secret HH:
Probably not. Most likely, they will give you
the information that leads to the services
that they feel they can provide to your child.

It's very important that you understand this, so that you know to look further than the information you get in the meeting and in the report. There are several reasons why this occurs. First, if the school recommends something, they generally have to provide it. As a rule, schools/districts do not provide everything students need. Second, we know from hundreds of off-the-record conversations with professionals on school teams, that they are often directed not to share information that will lead to excess costs for the school district.

Finally, most special education testing is completed for eligibility purposes. This means that, primarily, your child is tested to see if she qualifies for special education services, and not necessarily to uncover all the information about how she learns or what methods may work the best. If you feel that you are still lacking significant information, you can ask for that information and interpretation of the information. Be aware that you may need to seek your answers outside of the school.

46. What if the school district refuses my request for testing and an IEP?

Find a person who can help you advocate for your child. Gather all the information you have that shows your child is not making what you feel is reasonable progress in school. Next, in writing, request a meeting with the principal and teacher(s), and include your child's advocate. You may want to invite someone from your district's special education administration. At this meeting, show the school the information you have gathered, and ask that they evaluate your child for special education. Make this request verbally and also in writing.

Secret II:
Writing and dating the request is generally
the key to getting the evaluation.

If this does not work, request a meeting with the special education director, and again, give that person the written request. Be sure to keep accurate notes, dates, and the names of people that you communicate with, as this information may prove to be invaluable further into the process. According to a letter from the US Department of Education, even a student taking AP (Advanced Placement) classes in high school could be eligible for an IEP, so being smart and accomplished has nothing to with a denial.

Again, if the district denies your request to evaluate your child, it must provide you with your due process rights which you should read carefully. Basically, they would have to take you to due process, and as one special ed director told me, "That's a lot more expensive than an evaluation, so we generally don't do that."

47. What is the best way to go about having my child tested for learning disabilities in the public school system if she goes to a private school?

The Individual with Disabilities Education Act (IDEA) includes information about Child Find. This requires all school districts to identify, locate, and evaluate all children with disabilities, whether or not they are in public school. Evaluations take place at no cost to the family. Different school districts handle testing children in different ways: some with the Child Find team, others in the neighborhood schools, and others with a central testing team. So, contact the school district in which your daughter attends school and ask how to get her evaluated in that district and who evaluates a child in a private school, as this can vary from state to state.

If the team finds a disability and your daughter is not in public school, she may or may not be eligible for special education services from the district. School districts and states are allowed to decide how much and which services they will provide to children who do not receive public education. You should be able to receive this information in writing.

We recommend that you provide information from the staff at your daughter's current school, and that you invite at least one of your child's current teachers to the meeting, at which the results and recommendations will be discussed. If your child does end up receiving special education or related services from a school district, the district will need to ensure participation by the private school in service planning.

48. How can someone get diagnosed with dyslexia?

The simple answer is by a psychologist. However, it should be noted that there are many definitions and descriptions of dyslexia, or a reading disability. There are other professionals, or teams of professionals, who can discover whether or not your child has a reading disability. Many school districts hesitate to write "dyslexia" as the area of disability, but will categorize it as a specific learning disability. The trickiest piece is the lack of one definition of dyslexia that is used across the board. According to the International Dyslexia Association,

> *Dyslexia is a language-based learning disability. Dyslexia refers to a cluster of symptoms, which result in people having difficulties with specific language skills, particularly reading. Students with dyslexia usually experience difficulties with other language skills such as spelling, writing, and pronouncing*

words…It is referred to as a learning disability because dyslexia can make it very difficult for a student to succeed academically in the typical instructional environment, and in its more severe forms, will qualify a student for special education, special accommodations, or extra support services.

According to one of my neuropsychologist contacts, generally, to give a diagnosis of dyslexia or a reading disability, you need:

• Family history of reading weakness,

• Discrepancy between IQ and reading achievement,

• Weaknesses in auditory memory, auditory sequencing, or phonological processing, and current problems with reading and spelling,

It is crucial to diagnose and treat dyslexia as early as possible. Untreated, dyslexia can lead to low self-esteem, behavioral and social problems, and other issues.

For more information about dyslexia and its effects, read Sally Shaywitz' book *Overcoming Dyslexia.* Online resources are: International Dyslexia Association's website at *www.interdys.org*, Schwab Learning's website at *www.schwablearning.org* and the Wrightslaw's website about the diagnosis of dyslexia through DNA testing at *www.wrightslaw.com/news/05/dyslexia.genes.test.htm*.

All that said, the school can make an educational diagnosis of a reading disorder of some type on the determination form, using the federal and state categories.

49. Why is it so hard to convince the school to test my daughter to see if she qualifies for an IEP when she has been diagnosed with Attention Deficit Disorder (ADD)?

This is not uncommon. To be eligible for special education, your daughter needs to have a disability (ADD in her case) which affects her ability to learn from regular education services alone. There has to be an educational impact from the disability. Attention Deficit Disorder on its own is not enough. Usually schools are reluctant to evaluate students if they don't see any problems at school. Has the school said that they feel that your daughter is doing fine academically? Can you show them anything that suggests she is not? This can include work samples, conversations you've had with your daughter (a recording, perhaps), report cards, teacher conferences, etc.

Sometimes schools don't see the problems in the same way parents do. You may be spending hours fighting over homework and wearing yourself out trying to keep your daughter organized; the school may not know this. Record everything you are doing to keep your daughter on track along with the length of time that the homework takes, as it may be helpful in explaining to the school. If you have put your request in writing and the school/district still refuses, you might see if your daughter would qualify for a 504 plan instead. In some situations, parents wonder whether to take the risk of stopping all assistance to their child, and letting the child fail, in order to demonstrate to the school that the child needs help. There is no easy answer to this.

Not every child qualifies for special education services or a 504 plan. Even if your daughter does qualify, there is a good chance she will not get everything she needs to succeed academically, even if the school tells you that she will. Note that if the school staff tells you honestly what they really think your child needs, they may be required to provide it, especially if your child qualifies for special education. They may instead "downsize" her needs to fit the resources they have. You may need to advocate for more or different services, and/or you may need to decide how to get your child the additional help she needs outside of the public school system.

Secret JJ:
A school can "educationally diagnose" a child with ADD or ADHD. This now falls under the category of OHI – Other Health Impaired.   And, although they don't need it to qualify a child, if they insist that you take your child to the doctor or have the doctor write a report or fill out forms, you can request that they pay for that. I've seen more requests like that disappear when it's going to cost the district.

Sign Up Here For Your Free Gift
Be sure to sign up right now for the free video
series by going to www.getieptips.com . The tips
address the answers to the most common how-to
questions about the results you are seeking when
it comes to your child learning. There are
twenty-one 2 - 3 minute videos included.

Chapter Eleven: Friends

All You Need Is Love & Friendship!

 **Hi Yael, My 7th grader is getting bullied at school. He is on an IEP. Do I have any recourse? Please call me.**

50. Why does the school think that having friends is not important to my middle school child? Isn't learning how to negotiate relationships the most important skill in life?

Schools often focus on academics because they feel they know how to deliver this to most kids, and the link between social skills and academic progress can often be missed. I think that teachers can also feel at a loss about how to help a child make and keep friends, and that is why they tend to focus on other, more tangible things.

Having friends is more than a life skill; it is a fundamental human need. Studies show that people with friends get sick less often and recover more quickly from illness. School is stressful for most kids and stress impacts the immune system. Having friends may help reduce stress and boost the immune system, which will keep your kids healthier, as well as happier. This adds up to fewer school days lost to illness.

In addition, research into employment of adults with disabilities shows that it is a lack of social skills, and not difficulty learning the job, that typically leads to people being fired. Making and keeping friends in school means learning and using the social skills needed in the workplace.

Some colleagues of mine did some "research" of their own on this topic, and asked several middle school age kids what they like most about school. Four answered "Seeing my friends" and the fifth said, "Nothing is good about school; it's all hard work." We asked the fifth kid if anything makes up for the hard work, and guess what? He said seeing friends is the only thing that makes it bearable. Some kids added that friends are handy when you need to call someone to find out what the homework is. So, the teachers mostly concentrate on academics and the kids on friendship. But the most interesting of all the responses was the one from the sixth child, who responded, "Having friends is how you stay safe." We asked what he meant and he said that if you have friends, they look out for you and keep you from being bullied or getting depressed. This is crucial, considering that bullying and depression are major issues in our schools these days.

Secret KK:
Bullying can also be a denial of Special Education FAPE – free appropriate public education. It should never be tolerated and you should insist that it not be!
And no, your child should not be the one forced to switch schools.

This is the crux of the issue. Humans evolved to live in groups so that we could be safe in a hostile world (a bit like middle school). For this to happen, we needed to learn social skills to work cooperatively towards a common goal. Without this "team" around us, we are less productive, we get depressed, we don't feel safe, and we may not behave in safe ways. And if someone thinks this doesn't affect a child's education, it is hard to imagine what does.

51. How do I get the school to take my son's social and communication challenges seriously, get him the services he needs, and measure the outcomes in a meaningful way? He has high functioning autism.

This can be a frustrating process. The first step is to make sure you have a really good evaluation of your son's strengths and needs around social communication. This is typically done by a speech language professional in the school, but as they do not seem to be taking this seriously, you may need to seek a private therapist. If you already have private evaluations, that could help; provide these to the school as they must consider them. It is possible that the school feels that your son's deficits do not stop him from learning in school, so focus on why you think they do.

Once you have an evaluation that shows what skills your son has, and does not have, you can work with the school to decide what targeted skills your child needs to learn next in order to address any deficits. There are a variety of approaches – some research-driven and others not; I generally prefer the school uses those that are research-based. Choosing how and what skills to teach your child, and to help him generalize them to use with other children, will depend on your child's specific needs and age.

The team should then develop some appropriate goals for your son to achieve in the next year. These goals need to be very specific and measurable. I like to imagine we are in the classroom and have e team visualize what behaviors we will actually see when the child is using the targeted skills. This is the time to ask the regular education teacher(s) how this will look. The team needs to agree how progress will be evaluated and discuss what and how the data will be gathered.

Please read Question 50 on friendship for ideas to use in encouraging the school to take social/communication needs seriously. Also, read Chapter 8, Curriculum and Methodology, to learn about requesting an Independent Educational Evaluation (IEE) at district expense. If the school continues to resist acknowledging and working on his social/communication skills, you may want to take an advocate to your next meeting.

52. Our son has just started middle school. Instead of being in one classroom, he is now in eight different classes. In addition, his friends from elementary school don't want to "hang with him" any longer because he is different. What can the school do to help maintain these friendships?

The world of middle school is very different from elementary school. The emphasis for all kids is on fitting in socially. This often has the effect of isolating some kids from their familiar friends, because it isn't "cool" to hang out with anyone whom your new friends think is "different." In ad-

LONDON PUBLIC LIBRARY
20 EAST FIRST STREET
LONDON OH 43140

dition, it is very typical for kids to move to middle school and not hang out with old friends any more, and parents never really know why. However, it could feel quite different if your son has even just a couple of friends, whether they are old ones or new ones. The good news is that there are more potential friends in a bigger school; the key in middle and in high school is finding common interests and building upon them.

If your son has an Individualized Education Plan (IEP), you can ask to meet with the team and discuss your concerns about social isolation. If your son does not have an IEP and is in general education classes only, you might like to meet with the counselor or assistant principal. Make sure they know how important this is to you and your son, and ask for their ideas. You can ask that they try to put your son in classes with old friends, and that they also try to match him with kids who share some of his interests. Find out if there is a club or two that your son is interested in and can join. Some counselors also run "friendship groups" under a variety of names; this is a time both to learn and practice friendship skills, but also often a good place to make friends. You may want to find out if your district has what is generally known as an Inclusion Specialist; even if your child does not have an IEP, this person may be able to help.

Although beginning middle school is a difficult transition for almost all kids, and although the school system may tell you that these difficulties will help build character and prepare him for the real world, in the real world, your son has the right to expect to have friends. Many parents enroll their kids into after-school clubs like Scouts or other interest groups, as the friendships often seem to work better out of school. This may sustain your son while, hopefully, things in school settle down as the year wears on. Finding a place in the complicated social world of middle school definitely can be one of life's greatest challenges.

53. My child is in 9th grade and is fully included in regular education. She was recently the target of bullies, who physically assaulted her at the water fountain during the passing period. She was very upset and intimidated, and cried on and off for two days. have decided not to send her back to this school and have asked for homebound services, as I feel the school is unable to provide her with a safe environment. I have requested an IEP meeting to discuss her educational services and no one has responded. Do you have any suggestions?

This is very frightening. Above all, our kids should be safe in school. Clearly, it is the school's responsibility to provide a bully-free environment. The lack of response from the school is very concerning, as they do not seem to be taking this seriously. Since you have not received any response to your situation from the school, we suggest that you immediately write a formal complaint to the principal, the special education director, and the superintendent, telling them that you want an IEP meeting immediately. If they don't respond, or even if they do, we recommend that you do not go to the meeting alone and that you have an advocate (or even an attorney) present.

We believe your child should receive a significant amount of hours per day for homebound services, including possible therapy to deal with the attack. Know that there is no hard and fast rule about how many hours of homebound instruction a student can receive. In a situation like this, it is also important to contact the police, both to see if they can help keep your daughter safe and also to check about pursuing charges.

See *uniquelygifted.org/bullying.htm* for resources on the subject. And recently, the U.S. Education Department's Office for Civil Rights (OCR) issued a guidance letter to schools reminding them that bullying is wrong and must not be tolerated. It includes a reference to the delivery of FAPE for kids on IEPs and its relationship if bullying should occur. You can find it at *www2.ed.gov/about/offices/list/ocr/letters/colleague-bullying-201410.pdf*

Sign Up Here For Your Free Gift
Be sure to sign up right now for the free video series by going to www.getieptips.com . The tips address the answers to the most common how-to questions about the results you are seeking when it comes to your child learning. There are twenty-one 2 - 3 minute videos included.

Chapter Twelve: Accommodations

Leveling the Playing Field So Every Child Can Score a Goal

Hello Yael, Why is it so hard to get accommodations for my son? The school seems to think he doesn't need anything and that it's cheating if he has any. Am I missing something? Please contact me.

54. I need some examples of accommodations for our daughter's IEP. She is in seventh grade, has Attention Deficit Disorder (ADD), Obsessive-Compulsive Disorder (OCD), and Learning Disabilities (LD/PC/SLD) in reading and math. She is also gifted. In previous years, teachers were giving her extended time on homework, mostly because she couldn't locate the work when it was due. This year, teachers are penalizing her for late work, even if she turns it in later the same day it is due. We can't seem to get her teachers to give her any leeway, and this is causing her grades to go from A's to B's and C's.

It must be so hard to watch your daughter's grades fall despite her gifts and hard work. I imagine your daughter must be working a good deal harder than her classmates to overcome her challenges. From your description, your daughter probably has difficulties: keeping her attention on tasks, managing or even being aware of time, staying organized, managing anxiety and the OCD behaviors, reading (and maybe writing too), and performing math. Additional stress is going to make everything more difficult.

It is important to get the accommodations formalized into a 504 plan or an IEP, because this is the only way to get them enforced in school. There is a terrific resource online entitled "Twice Exceptional Students, Gifted Students with Disabilities: An Introductory Resource Book" that you can download from Colorado's Department of Education at: *www.cde.state.co.us/sites/default/files/documents/gt/download/pdf/twiceexceptionalresourcehandbook.pdf.* Most of the information applies nationally, not just to Colorado. A 2007 opinion letter from OSEP (Office of Special Education Programs) explains about the rights gifted children have to special education and 504 plans, even when taking accelerated courses: *www.ed.gov/about/offices/list/ocr/letters/colleague-20071226.html.* More great information about gifted children with disabilities can be found by searching *www.wrightslaw.com.*

Secret LL:
You can be in honors classes and still have an IEP.

Examples of Accommodations

- Reminders of passage of time: Regular time checks from teachers, or a watch on her desk.

- Building small deadlines into assignments, to help with keeping track of longer-term time management.

- Having just one file folder, with work to be submitted that day, to take to class.

- Extended time, in case a deadline is accidentally missed, for reading, comprehending, and producing written materials, and to help reduce anxiety.

- Teacher support with breaking assignments down into parts, to help with organizing written work.

- Excellent home-school communication is absolutely essential.

- Student and parents will both be provided with exactly what the expectations are for all assignments, including deadlines, so you can help at home.

- Use of a calculator for math.

- Written examples of math problems which show the structured process taught in class for working them out.

- Abbreviated assignments – that does not mean different work, just less of it. This means three paragraphs instead of five, or ten math problems instead of twenty.

- Audiobooks/Audiotextbooks: See *www.learningally.org* or *www.bookshare.org* for information. Many school districts hold licenses for use when this is included in an IEP or 504 plan. Sometimes there are grants from the State Department of Education for families to access these.

- Copies of notes, or a lesson plan, with key words highlighted to help her take her own set of organized notes.

- Pre-teaching of new vocabulary words.

- An extra copy of all textbooks to keep at home.

- Homework buddy system, or access to the school Homework Line, and agreement from administration that teachers will post assignments.

- An adult she trusts at school, whom she can talk to if she needs help on the "inside" with getting teachers to make accommodations.

Secret MM:
The one accommodation that almost everyone tries to get is extra time – on homework, classwork, etc. This is the one I don't like, except on tests, or something due at the end of class. The reason is that when a child gets behind, it all just snowballs. I've known so many kids who get to the end of the semester, and there just is no way they can catch up. In my experience, shortened assignments are a much better arrangement.

---

55. My son is a 6th grader w/ chronic asthma. Last year, he was out of school for 41 days. I worry with middle school looming (and the amount of in-class instruction he misses). Will he qualify for IDEA/ special education?

Middle school is a worry for many parents, even without the extra concern you have. We suggest you start by meeting with your child's treating physician. Discuss the situation at school and the specific criteria for when your child needs to stay home. In another situation we are aware of, this decision is made by the mother on a day-by-day basis. Her decision is based upon the flow meter reading at which the physician has indicated that the child's asthma is acute enough to remain home. At a minimum, the school needs to have a Health Care and Emergency Plan in place for your child.

Your child may or may not qualify for an IEP. It depends upon whether the missed days in school have resulted in him being so far behind academically, that he is unable to access the curriculum due to gaps in his learning. In order to see if your son qualifies for special education services, he will need to be tested by the school for eligibility. Your son's physician's recommendations must be taken into consideration during this process. (Alarming as it seems, missing even large amounts of time and content in school for any reason is not necessarily a guarantee that the child will qualify for special education services.) If your son does not qualify for special education, he may qualify under 504/ADA guidelines. This, again, is a decision that has to be made by a team of people, which includes you and the school. If your son is eligible under 504, you could discuss the following accommodations with the school: modified attendance policies, modified school day, strategies to make up for lost instruction if he misses a lot of school, alternative options for instruction when out of school, modified activity level for P.E., and administration of any medications needed. Using available technology, like webcams, microphones, the internet, and even robots in some districts, your child (although not well enough to leave home) may be able to participate in classes even when he is not physically present in school. (The newest robots are ipads on wheels.)

56. Are service dogs for children with autism allowed in the school?

In recent years, there have been articles in newspapers around the country on this issue, and you should probably surf the internet to see what both the obstacles and successes are. You will definitely need a letter from your child's doctor stating the need for a service dog in school. The service dog should be put into the IEP as an accommodation. Some schools may allow a service dog for a trial period, and if so, data should be collected and no other changes should be made while the trial is going on.

Although I have not personally come across therapy dogs for children with autism in schools, I have experience of dogs improving accessibility for children with other types of disabilities. It is important to have the people who trained the dog go into the school and make sure the dog is properly trained for the school environment. It is helpful if the trainer can meet and "train" some of the school staff, so they know what to teach the other adults and kids about how to behave around the service dog. Even though this seems to be new ground for many schools, each time it comes up, they will need some help.

"4 Paws for Ability" is one organization which trains service dogs for children with autism; their website *www.4pawsforability.org* contains some success stories about dogs attending schools, how parents made that happen, and what they learned from the data. One of the common objections is about other children who are severely allergic to dogs; if this is the case, obviously the adults will need to figure out a solution. There are some great articles about the benefits of dogs and we suggest you check out the book *Healing Power of Pets* by Dr. Marty Becker, D.V.M. And for excellent dog training and care, you might want to check out *FalcoK9academy.com.*

57. If my child can only go to school for half a day, is the district required to help me provide the parts of the curriculum she's missing?

There are plenty of students who cannot, for one reason or another, spend a full day in school. It sounds like this is the case for your daughter. In such situations, a shortened day is discussed and agreed upon by the IEP team, and it is usually written into the IEP as an accommodation. So, if the IEP team has agreed to this accommodation, it makes sense that the school has some responsibility for ensuring that your daughter gets a similar education to the other kids who stay a full day at school. Special education services are provided so that your daughter can learn from the general education curriculum. This includes all the parts of instruction she is missing when she is not in school.

There are many creative ways to do this at home: dinner time discussions, field trips with parents, videos, special projects, and library books. The most important thing is that someone at the school needs to communicate to you, on an ongoing basis, what the gaps are for each subject area, and help you with some ideas and possibly the materials to complete them. This task usually falls to the special education teachers, as they are in the best position to gather curriculum and materials from all the other teachers. They can also make any modifications needed and discuss them with you. A combination of school/homebound services might be possible as well as a robot. See the answer to Question 55.

I suggest that you request a meeting to identify the gaps in your daughter's education and have a written agreement about how to fill them. As you and the special education teacher are a limited resource, the plan needs to be realistic or it probably won't happen.

Sign Up Here For Your Free Gift
Be sure to sign up right now for the free video series by going to www.getieptips.com . The tips address the answers to the most common how-to questions about the results you are seeking when it comes to your child learning. There are twenty-one 2 - 3 minute videos included.

Ocean's Apart? Bring Your Ships Together

Hi Yael, There seems to be a huge disconnect between the school and me. My daughter is unable to bring home the homework assignments or she brings them home, but doesn't know what to do. I've asked the school over and over for this information, but they don't seem to want to do it. How do I convince them? They are complaining I am taking too much of their time. But by the time I add up the hours of conversations we have about this, they could have done this in a third of that time!

58. My child gets speech and occupational therapy services at school. I never have direct communication with the providers and I have no idea what happens in the sessions. Can I ask to see their therapy notes?

Have you asked to speak with the therapists? That would likely be the first move as therapy notes may be unhelpful (they often record amount of time and little else), and we've found that for some reason, requesting them can upset some therapists; many are fine with it. At this point, you want to focus on starting a relationship with the therapists so you and they can talk directly. Start the process carefully. Leave a note at the school, send an email, or ask the special education teacher how to make this happen. In your message, let the therapists know that you'd like to reinforce what they do at school at home. Ask for ideas and suggestions from them, and also ask if you could come and observe a session, and/or meet with them for a few minutes afterwards.

It is also important to have the IEP indicate how, and how often, you will receive progress reports on IEP goals, as this is another way you can get updated on your child's progress with the skills the OT and speech therapist are working on. Be sure you get this added to your child's IEP at the next meeting because you need this information to fully participate in modifying goals.

If you ask the therapists specifically what they are doing after telling them you would like to support their work with your child at home — and then do that, hopefully the therapists will understand you are not out to get them , but to work collaboratively.

59. How do I convey that I would like to be treated with respect at my child's IEP meetings? I feel like they think I am stupid.

This is a very common problem and I hear this much too often. Sometimes, the right approach can produce wonderful results. First, figure out what behavior you would like see in the other people if they were showing you respect. Be specific and list them. You certainly want to make sure that you set up some ground rules based on this list for the next meeting. Some examples are: you will be able to speak without interruption, what you say will be written down, your questions will be answered, and if anyone has anything to say, he or she will say it directly. Ask that everyone at the meeting keeps in mind that the goal is to create a successful educational environment for your child; you may want to bring a large photo of your child and set it upon the table.

Secret NN:
When I attend a meeting and observe eye-rolling or sighing, I often turn immediately to the person and say something like, "I can see from your body language that something I just said has had an impact on you; can you please share what you are thinking?"

Also, make sure that you are well prepared before going into the meeting. Ask, in writing, that any documents the school is drafting be given to you a week before the meeting. (Even with this request, you'll often get them just a day or so before the meeting, but even this can be helpful.) List your goals for and questions about your child, and make sure you reread the current IEP along with any new documents. Be as informed as possible before you walk into the meeting. Take a friend, family member, or advocate, so you won't feel outnumbered. That person can take notes for you, which will allow you to listen to and participate more effectively in the discussions.

Finally, read an article called "The Blame Game." After you read it, you may feel sad, but you won't feel so alone. The Wrights gave me permission to reprint it as it is one of my favorite articles to give both to parents and to school staffs. Check it out on my website, under Articles at specialediephelp.com or at wrightslaw.com/advoc/articles/ALESSI1.html.

60. My daughter has had an IEP since 3rd grade; she is now in 11th grade. It has come to my attention that in one of her classes, her IEP accommodations are not being provided. I feel like my daughter's rights have been violated. I had a meeting yesterday with the teacher, who claims he had no knowledge of my daughter's IEP or her accommodations. What are my rights as a parent of a child with an IEP?

Do you feel like the meeting yesterday resolved the problem with this particular teacher, and that he will provide accommodations in the future? If it did, you will still want to see if your daughter's grades in this class have been affected by the lack of accommodations. If they have, request a meeting to discuss this. You will want to include the class teacher, the special education teacher, and the principal in this discussion. At this meeting, you can also ask how this lack of communication regarding IEP accommodations can be avoided in the future. If you feel that the problem has not been resolved, you should request an immediate IEP meeting and discuss the situation there. Prior to the meeting, you should also check if the accommodations are in effect in her other classes.

If the problem is also occurring in her other classes, specifically ask for the attendance of all your daughter's regular education teachers at the IEP meeting. Make your request in writing to the special education teacher and be sure to include a copy to the principal and the regular education teachers involved. Remember to be polite, no matter how upset you are. Your daughter has the right to have all the accommodations in her IEP implemented in the classrooms. Remember that you are your child's ambassador to success, and the meeting will allow you the opportunity to make sure that all her teachers understand her needs and accommodations. If your daughter continues to be denied accommodations, you should seek legal advice. Feel free to contact me for referrals.

61. What does the district need to provide when the parents' mode of communication is not a written language?

School districts are required to make sure that all written information given to parents is translated verbally or by other means, and that the parents completely understand the information. There are agencies with translators and interpreters available if no one in the school district can communicate in the parents' language.

62. How can I get the school personnel to overlook their dislike of each other and come together to make educational decisions on behalf of my child?

Because you are dealing with people, unfortunately, you have no control over their complicated relationships with each other. You can try to speak to them individually and let them know that you are aware of the tension between some of the staff members. Empathize with their difficulties, and express that you really need them to come to the table with only one thought on their minds: working together to determine and provide the necessary services for your child's education. Be gracious and understanding, but make sure that they have heard your desires and understand your child's needs. You might also send each member a personal invitation to the meeting, saying you value and look forward to hearing their ideas. It may help to bring some food to create a more relaxed meeting. Try to stick to an agenda, because it will make the meeting flow more successfully. Good Luck!

63. I have just become a part of my grandson's IEP team. I have dealt with IEPs on and off for years. I don't have a good feeling about this school or his teachers. They don't seem to want anyone from the outside (me) to be involved. When I met with the special education teacher, my sense was that she wanted to let me know that she was in control of my grandson's education. How can I find someone to help me work with the school?

It is often difficult to make the IEP team members realize that you have your grandson's interests at heart and that you also have expertise as to what he needs. First, if you don't have legal guardianship, make sure to obtain a release of information from the person who is the parent or guardian. If you persist and try to work through the issues, perhaps your help will be appreciated by the school team, and your grandson's needs will be met. I have also met teachers who do not have wonderful social skills with adults, but who are wonderful with kids; that could be part of the problem.

You might want to try sending a note to the special education teacher, with a copy to the principal and the regular education teachers. Be gracious and polite, and write, "As I mentioned at the recent meeting, I will be an integral part of my grandson's educationally planning." Mention that you are hoping that you will all be able to work together for your grandson's benefit. In the letter, make one request (perhaps a copy of the file, or a time when you can come in and look at his files, or observe him in class), and see how they respond to your request. If they continue to attempt to distance you, we would recommend that you take a diplomatic advocate along with you to the next meeting.

Sign Up Here For Your Free Gift
Be sure to sign up right now for the free video series by going to www.getieptips.com . The tips address the answers to the most common how-to questions about the results you are seeking when it comes to your child learning. There are twenty-one 2 - 3 minute videos included.

Chapter Fourteen: Resources

If Your Ship Doesn't Come In, Swim Out To It

Hi Yael, What are they talking about now? They sent home a really incomprehensible IEP draft – talking about ambulation and a bunch of puzzles to figure out – BIP, ILP, RTI, something about scaffolding. Why can't they talk in English? Call me please, I need to know what to say.

64. How do I help my child with disabilities to learn and what are the most useful resources?

Contact me at *yael@getiephelp.com* or by calling me at (303) 800-4118. My website is specialediephelp.com and my facebook page is Get IEP Help. I'll be happy to discuss resources for your child's specific disabilities. I have a huge resource bank of knowledge and referrals from around the country that may benefit your child's particular situation. This information can save you hours of research and point you in the best directions. You can also contact your state department of education, or go online to its web site. You can also speak with other advocates, and search for resources online. Wrightslaw, at *www.Wrightslaw.com*, is an amazing website and I send parents there all the time, especially to order their parent educational books and webinars. Other websites that are helpful for finding resources are *www.Iser.com* and *www.ldonline.org.*

65. What do all those "Greek words" that they use at my child's IEP meetings mean?

Secret OO:
When staff uses jargon at the IEP,
ask what it means—each time.
Say "I'd really appreciate it if
you'd speak in plain English."
When I'm in a meeting,
I do this a lot for the parents.
Oh—and just when you get
used to the jargon, it will change.

Sign Up Here For Your Free Gift
Be sure to sign up right now for the free video
series by going to www.getieptips.com . The tips
address the answers to the most common how-to
questions about the results you are seeking when
it comes to your child learning. There are
twenty-one 2 - 3 minute videos included.

Appendix: Do It Yourself

Or Do I Really Need Help From An Advocate?

This book will get you through a number of the obstacles on your way to helping your child overcome his or her learning challenges. Child advocacy is not a mystery, and it is entirely possible for you to effectively advocate for your child. But often a special education advocate can save you time and get your child services that you don't even know exist. One parent I know recently commented that she had spent hours researching both the law and what kind of dyslexia services were available before she found me. Once I got involved, we focused in on what her child needed, and got it. Be sure to visit the next page for the checklist of attributes you'll be wanting if you get your child an advocate, as although many of us are excellent, according to those school staff who have confided in me, we are not all created equal. You want an advocate who can really help your child!

A Checklist for Choosing An Advocate

Here's what you're looking for, an advocate who . . .

- Shares your belief that your child can and deserves to learn

- Actually listens to what you think and know about your own child, and takes that into account

- Analyzes and explains all those reports you have

- Gives you a professional "second opinion" on what the school gave you

- Helps you understand the findings about your child in easy-to-understand language

- Creates an action plan and fallback options that can be put into place right now to get what you need for your child's education

- Helps with problem solving, and guides you to make the right decisions for your child

- Saves you time by giving you the list of things you need to gather, read, and do

- Advises you, so you know what to say and what not to say

- Acts as a shield for you and your child, so that if anyone at the meeting gets annoyed, it is directed at the advocate and not at you

- Helps you feel confident when you enter and participate in that next school meeting

- Can attend school meetings with you, either in person or through technology, no matter where in the country you live

- Has the education, the credentials, and track record to help you get your child's educational needs met.

Top 5 Things to Note

1. Don't say "best" but never forget that's exactly what you need for your child -- and your child deserves it.

2. When at all possible, it pays to resolve differences with the schools without delving into the legal system.

3. If it's not in writing (or at least on a recording), it's as if it didn't happen.

4. You MUST learn how to "play the game," or take someone with you who knows the rules. The school/district holds almost all the cards and chances are won't tell you the rules.

5. A knowledgeable and efficient advocate can get you things for your child that you didn't even realize existed. As numerous clients of mine have said: "Yael had me thinking of things I had never thought of...

NEVER FORGET!

A "no" about your child from a school district means

Come up with a different way to get the school or district

to say Yes!

So Don't Give Up!

77244523R00057

Made in the USA
Columbia, SC
23 September 2017